Pylgrim's Progress

How to be a
WINNER
in the
Global Knowledge Economy

Pylgrim's Progress

How to be a
WINNER
in the
Global Knowledge Economy

Tim Kidson and Sharon Niccolls
Tim Kidson & Associates

word4word design & publishing

Pylgrim's Progress: How to be a WINNER in the Global Knowledge
Economy
© Tim Kidson and Sharon Niccolls

A copy of this publication has been registered with the British
Library.

Published by Word4Word Design & Publishing
107 High Street
Evesham
Worcestershire
WR11 4EB
United Kingdom
www.w4wdp.com

Printed in the UK by Cromwell Press, Trowbridge

ISBN 0-9541209-7-3

Acknowledgements

We owe special thanks to:

Our many and varied clients; they are the source and inspiration for this book. They are the winners, each in their own special way.

Sue Froggatt of Sue Froggatt Training and Consulting who, during our very first chance meeting, said, 'You must write a book!' Sue has advised and guided us all along the way. It was Sue who made the link between tacit knowledge and the TK Factor™ business development process.

Richard Good of Frenchclasses.com: he not only read the first draft giving real thought and insight on how it could be improved, but read and helped amend all subsequent drafts as well.

Sue Richardson and Debbie Macmillan, partners in Word4Word, our publishers – Sue does the words and Debbie has an eye for the look and feel of the finished product; they both have great ideas!

Anne Harbour who used her lifetime of publishing experience to guide us from the very first draft.

Julie Milne, the 'third leg' of the TKA stool; assistant and confidante, who has offered unflinching support throughout the process.

We thank Business Link Herefordshire and Worcestershire where people like Mac Auld were always supportive towards our ideas; Craig Robinson and David Shelton set up some great training and development days and opportunities for the then adviser teams. These are people who always give so much more than they take.

This is where we met John McMahon of Forum 21 who first made us aware of the need for all organisations to move towards 'knowledge'. This book is concerned with the practical 'how to do it'.

And last but not least: our long-suffering children, who have lived the book with us and who are almost convinced that Ali Shah really exists!

To Emily, Jenny, Ursula and Alistair,
who are the future.

If your time to you
Is worth savin'
Then you better start swimmin'
Or you'll sink like a stone
For the times they are a changin'.

Bob Dylan
The Times They Are A-Changin'

Tim Kidson is a business development specialist, facilitator and inspirational speaker. He works with CEOs who want to be winners; senior people who wish to change their thinking, change their behaviour and change what they do in order to improve both themselves and their organisations.

Sharon Niccolls has a family business background and is well equipped to take a holistic view of businesses and organisational development in a range of sectors. She is a skilled trainer and facilitator, experienced in writing and delivering development programmes.

Contents

Introduction

We have both spent many years working with individuals and groups to help them fulfil their potential. We have worked with hundreds of organisations, from manufacturing to retail, tourism and agriculture, high tech to leasing, large and small, profit-making to funded bodies, councils and government departments. The main thing all these organisations have in common is that people deliver performance outcomes.

Pylgrim's Progress is the story of a once successful English family business that decided it wanted to become a winner in the global knowledge economy. Being a winner means creating and sustaining competitive advantage. Even a successful charity has to develop this mindset.

Running alongside the story is a commentary by a mythical adviser we have called Ali Shah. He represents a compilation of all the excellent advisers we have worked with. Hence he might seem a bit too good to be true! We have found that the demands and complexities of today's world mean that many of us look to hand chunks of our lives over to trusted external advisers. Who would seriously question the advice of their dental hygienist, their motor mechanic, their IT specialist or their website designer? Providing always that these relationships are based upon trust.

There are four stages to this journey, not just for Pylgrim's Porcelain Ltd and the individuals concerned, but for any organisation and its people that makes a similar commitment, anywhere in the world.

The first stage is for the leaders to agree on **the bull's eye**. A bull's eye is a metaphor for the answers to three specific questions on what the organisation could look like in, say, three years' time. Many organisational and personal development tools are agreed on one thing and that is the clearer we are about where we want to be or what we want to achieve the more likely we are to be successful. The bull's eye reveals the collective ambition of the leaders in an organisation.

The second stage is to discuss the increasing impact of knowledge on our lives. **What we buy** or hire, including people, is gradually, inevitably containing more and more knowledge. People are more flexible, more mobile and more intelligent than ever; successful people expect more from their life and their work. This always means that we need to see **what we do** differently in order to harness and maximise the value of this knowledge. The primary activities of the 'old' manufacturing economy were buying it, making it and selling it. We would suggest that the primary activities in the global knowledge economy are research and development, marketing, customer relationships and continued personal development from the top down. When we do things differently it will change the products and particularly the services we can offer; this will change **what we sell**.

The third stage is to look at the modern organisation. As weightless, microscopic information travels at 186,000 miles per second, we need to be aware that there are no safe havens for doing business anymore. We have to continuously scan the horizon for **new technologies** that could impact on or maybe destroy our business. The sheer speed of these changes means that we need to adopt **new management techniques**, always starting at the very top of an organisation. The 360° appraisal starting with the MD, for example, is one of the most powerful things an organisation can do to improve its culture. If the MD's development points are linked to the bull's eye and then published for the workforce to share, then quantum improvements in people performance can also start to move at the speed of light.

There is a direct link between this work and the **new strategies** that are necessary to meet increasing customer requirements of 'more value for less' and enhanced competitor capability. In a 24/7 world we need to adjust structures, systems, products and services, people, and salaries as fast as the market place demands. More than ever before we have to play the great game of business by the rules of economics, not prejudice, politics, outdated notions, or complacency.

The fourth and final stage is to acknowledge *intellectual capital* as the new asset for the new economy. It starts with our **structural capital** that includes our processes and procedures, our trademarks and patents; indeed any knowledge asset we can leverage for the benefit of our customers. These aspects of many organisations are in constant flux due to the impact of technology and therefore our **human capital** has to be improving too. Enhancing the skills (the how-to-do), knowledge (the what-to-do) and attitudes (the wanting-to-do) of everyone on the payroll is part of this work. Making continuous personal development for all not just a mantra, but a habit, is part of the journey towards excellence.

The final element of the final stage concerns **customer capital**. When we come up against world-class competition, it will be what our customers think of our performance that counts. The better the quality of relationships with stakeholders and internal and external customers the better will be the performance of our business. We need not only to measure customer capital, but to be constantly trying to enhance it.

For example, as we wrote *Pylgrim's Progress* we ran a series of 10 seminars under the heading, 'How to Be a WINNER in the Global Knowledge Economy' for 10 local company directors. Each of the sessions mirrored the 10 chapters of this book. We asked them to evaluate the course using a variety of criteria. Our scores were 85 percent overall and this together with their comments is the basis for improving the next director development programmes we run.

So this work is not intended to be prescriptive; we have discovered that there are no quick fixes, no magic bullets. None of the models, none of the learning points, none of Ali's recommendations are answers in themselves, though we believe that they are part of an answer. This is a 'pick and mix' selection box where there will be something for everyone who is responsible for improving organisational performance.

So why did we write it?

We, and every one of our clients, work in a global

knowledge economy, where customers sometimes want more for less, where competitors can appear from nowhere and technology-driven market places are changing as we speak. This reality means that we increasingly need an 'outside in' perspective on our organisation, on what we do, and even on ourselves.

The problem is, however, that all our experience of the world to date has been from the 'inside out'. Individually, we experience everything in the first instance through our five senses of sight, sound, smell, taste and touch. We are programmed from birth to see everything from 'first' position, our own views, our own perspectives. And this worked well enough in the 'old' manufacturing economy, where demand exceeded supply, quotas, tariffs and the fixed assets on the balance sheet were the key to generating profit. A reactive paradigm worked well enough for most in those days.

In order to develop and sustain competitive advantage in the global economy – where knowledge is the new asset – we have to learn to see the world from 'second' position. We have to get closer to our customers than ever before, we have to benchmark ourselves against world-class competitors, we have to adapt our offering to the changing demands of the market place. Essentially this means being proactive.

In our work, we sometimes use a sequence that can help us with this. A 'trigger' experience is something that happens, causing us to think. When we think about that experience, we can make decisions and the decisions we make can lead to action. We all have trigger experiences but we all think, decide and act in a unique manner, using our tacit knowledge, the stuff that lives inside our heads.

Because of the speed of change in the world, there are a lot of trigger experiences available to anyone that runs a business today. Therefore the think, decide, act sequence requires a further element to be successful and that is transparency. This does not mean telling everyone everything, but it does mean sharing information that materially affects our progress.

We have to communicate and listen more effectively than ever, both individually and collectively, with the three groups of people that we need to apply this process to. The first group are our internal customers, that is, everyone on the payroll. The second group are our external customers, that is, the people that pay us. The third group are our stakeholders, that is, anyone materially involved with the organisation.

There is a risk with transparency. It can lead to closer, better quality relationships with the key people that have an impact on our organisation. It can also lead to a parting of the ways; it may just speed up an inevitable process. The steeper the gradient on the flight path towards the bull's eye, the more important the quality of our people, our customers and our stakeholders becomes. Some people, for a great variety of reasons, may simply want something different.

So we believe that the unique tacit knowledge that everyone in an organisation possesses must be harnessed. The TK Factor™ business development process is the conscious identifying, using and enhancing of tacit knowledge leading initially to transparency with others, and ultimately to business reward. This is how to develop the intellectual capital of any organisation, the new asset for creating and sustaining competitive advantage in the global knowledge economy.

Tim Kidson
Sharon Niccolls
Hereford, March 2005
kidson@growth-for-business.com
www.growth-for-business.com

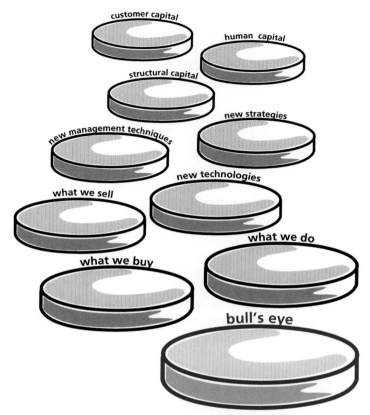

Chapter One: The Bull's Eye

Pylgrim's Porcelain Ltd manufactures and distributes table and giftware. The company has been trading for 28 years and was set up by John Pylgrim. In addition to the production of traditionally made dinner services, now manufactured in China, there is a small manufacturing part of the business remaining in the UK, which is unprofitable. In the early 1990s, the company employed 60 people, now it employs 30. The business has invested quite heavily in technology that allows them to design and decorate the whiteware they import.

John's son, Robert, is 32. He joined the company four years

ago following his Business Studies degree and various stints with other companies. He has spent much of this time commuting to China in order to set up the contacts with manufacturers. Last year he returned to the UK, ostensibly to take up the role of MD from his father. Robert has heard of a business consultant by the name of Ali Shah who was very helpful in bringing about change in a friend's company…

"You've got a *what* coming in?"

"A consultant, Dad."

"A consultant!"

Robert Pylgrim remained silent as his father tried to pace the confines of the cupboard that had been allocated to Robert as his 'office' on his return to the fold of the family business six months previously.

"And just who is this consultant?"

"Someone Geoff Short recommended – Ali Shah."

"A woman!"

"He's a bloke, Dad – and very highly thought of!"

'Ahem…Excuse me gentlemen…' Robert glanced up to see his father's secretary of 12 years, Ruth Ellison, standing in the doorway.

"John – that rep is here to see you –and has been waiting in your office for 20 minutes now!"

"Alright, alright, I'm coming woman – don't rant! We'll continue this discussion later, boy!"

John Pylgrim strode from the room in a tightly strung tornado of suppressed and frustrated energy.

Robert sighed and spared a moment to pity the rep, who would no doubt feel the effects of his father's irritation.

Ruth came into the room.

"I am very fond of your father as you know, but I don't think he knows the meaning of the phrase 'politically correct'."

"I know, Ruthie – though at 67 he is probably far too old to change."

"I gather he didn't take kindly to the idea of having this management consultant coming in – but you know what he is like – just give him a bit of time to get used to the idea and he'll be fine. I'm afraid he's not finding it at all easy to hand over the reins – bless him!"

"That's all very well, Ruth, but I'm not sure how much longer I can cope with this situation. He lured me back from China with the promise of making me MD – and like an idiot I thought it would work. I may be many things in this company but I am not an MD! Just because he plays golf every Friday and tells everyone I am in charge does not mean I am – the staff all still go to him for major decisions – and look at this office! It's a bloody joke!"

"He just needs time to adjust."

"Well as far as I am concerned he has had all the time he is getting. This consultant will make or break it. I've worked really hard over the last five years to get this company out of the trouble it was in. I spent all that time in the Far East sourcing the right manufacturers for our porcelain and look at the thanks I get! If Dad won't be persuaded then I shall have to rethink my position here."

"Well I don't recommend you give him an ultimatum, you know how obstinate he can be when he wants to be," said Ruth.

"Don't worry; I've got a few tricks up my sleeve to persuade him. I just wish he was bit more, you know, excited about the things I've done to try and change things here. He seems to vacillate from trying to hang on to his authority to moments when he seems to have just given up. I don't know what to do and I need some help – outside help. Everyone here is just too close to the situation."

"He is pleased, I know he is – he just likes to remember the hay days when he had loads of people working for him. I think he feels that he has failed in some way – now that we are so small."

Robert never thought of his father as a failure – he had worked so hard to set the business up, build it into something local people respected and he had survived through some sticky times, even the latest crisis of the declining manufacturing base in this country. He looked at Ruth and considered this example of her insight and perception. He was so used to thinking of her as his Dad's secretary that when she came out with these nuggets she often took him by surprise.

"We had to streamline, Ruth, you know that – this is a global economy we are now working in and we would have gone bust if we had tried to retain full manufacture here. We'd no choice. At least we are now solvent and our designs are getting more recognition."

Robert paused for a moment and frowned.

"It's just…"

Ruth looked at him expectantly.

"It's just what?"

"Well I know in theory we've done the right thing but what scares me most is how I sustain it. Where do I go from here with it? At 32 you'd have thought I'd have a better idea – if I am honest that is another reason why I want this consultant in. The old ways of doing things are no longer valid and I need to learn some new ways before it's too late. I'm not sure Dad is the right role model for the new business age."

***

Two days later Robert was again behind his desk. He felt frazzled. In his visitor's chair was an immaculately dressed man, composed and calm regarding Robert with a somewhat enigmatic expression.

"I really am sorry, Ali – I didn't mean to subject you to the full wrath of my father."

"It's really no problem, Robert – I am very used to being met with anything from scepticism to total hostility. Your father did at least shake my hand and has not shown me the door. Yet." He grinned. "We'll find a way to work together once we've overcome his natural fear and he understands the real value of what he's buying."

"Lord yes! I thought he was going to have an apoplexy when you told him your day rate! I think you'll be of enormous help to us, though."

Ali bowed his head in acknowledgement.

"The first step we need to take is to agree a bull's eye for the business."

"How do you mean?"

"Well, we'll need to decide where you as a company want the business to be in three years' time. I use the metaphor of a bull's eye, a target if you like, so that having established it, we can then decide upon the flight path – in other words how you'll get there."

"But isn't this just like one of those vague, meaningless mission statements that so many organisations have and ignore?"

"Indeed not, the bull's eye has several features – the first is that it's very precise and will answer three key questions; the second is that there are numbers attached so it has a meter to measure, so to speak; the third is that it'll identify the specific areas of the business that need to be concentrated on, to change what you are doing in order to achieve it; and finally the process of establishing the bull's eye will involve all your key players, who'll not only decide and agree on the bull's eye but will also sign it off to confirm their commitment to it."

"So we need to set up a meeting with the senior management team?"

"That would be an excellent idea – I suggest we set a day aside for this and go off site so there are no interruptions."

"And after that, what'll we do? As you know, one of the things that rang a bell with me when I spoke to Geoff Short about the work you'd done with him was this whole idea of functioning in the global economy. Just not sure I entirely know what that actually means!" Robert confessed.

"Well let's consider what John said about my day rate."

Robert groaned. "Look, his bark is worse than his bite – I know he didn't mean to be so insulting…"

Ali just laughed, "Believe me I've been called many worse things in my time, don't concern yourself. But let's consider the concept of 'What we buy' in the context of the global economy."

"How do you mean?"

Ali reached into his pocket and drew out a handful of smooth, flat pebbles. He placed them on the desk.

"Imagine, if you will Robert, that part of our work together will be like creating a path." He pushed the pebbles gently around on the desk with a long, elegant finger. He spread them into a rough pattern. "We are creating a path – some stepping-stones if you like – which will enable you to cross the turbulent waters of the river in comparative safety. The bank we are on is the present. We can turn our heads and see the past stretching behind us. The river is the new global economy and the opposite bank is our future, the new world. The stepping-stones are the way in which we get there – they are how we build competitive advantage."

"And I suppose the bull's eye is somewhere on the opposite bank is it, nailed to a tree?"

Ali smiled, "Indeed it is and these ten pebbles represent the ten stages to you getting there. The key is how you take each step and move from stone to stone. Your success may also lie in how brave you are in pushing forward and how determined you are to succeed. The journey may not be easy…"

He looked at Robert.

"Your father has questioned my value and rightly so. The value of explicit knowledge is going down – the computer you buy today will be not only cheaper but better than the one you bought last year. But the value of tacit knowledge…" Ali tapped his head gently, "…the value of tacit knowledge – what only I know or can do, or what only you know or can do – is going up. The key, my friend, is to know what value to put on it and how you use it in your business. That is what will make you real winners!"

Robert smiled for the first time that day.

"I can't wait to get started," he said.

The Bull's Eye: Roadmap for Action

Ali Shah has been advising a variety of organisations for many years. He is actively involved with some 40 clients around the UK all of whom, without exception, are having to look at just about everything they do from a fresh perspective. Pylgrim's is typical of a company that needs to fundamentally change its thinking from what was successful in the 'old' manufacturing economy to what will be necessary in the 'new' global knowledge economy. Ali does not mince words.

The trigger experience...

At an awards dinner some time ago, Matthew Pinsent, the Olympic gold medallist said that his team's bull's eye was very simple. In the four years between the Atlanta Olympics and the Sydney Olympics they needed to be able to row the distance four seconds faster.

He said they knew that if they could achieve that feat they would win gold again. He went on to describe what this challenge really meant to the members of his team, the commitments and the sacrifices, to work towards a world-beating bull's eye.

Clearly the model still worked in Athens 2004 too!

...this experience leads to thoughts...

Make the time to produce a bull's eye with your senior people. It can be a trigger experience. Start at the beginning. *What* do you want to be? In the global knowledge economy it is an even more fundamental question for all organisations to ask. The clearer we are about where or what we want to achieve the more likely we are to be successful.

Produce your bull's eye with your senior management team (SMT) by answering four questions:

What do we want to be? Define your products and services in 10 words.

For whom? Define the customers you want in six words.

How much? This can be sales and profit. For a trade association it could be membership. For a UK school, it could be an Ofsted grade.

By when? Agree a date, usually three years on.

See 'How to hit the bull's eye' on the opposite page.

...thoughts lead to decisions and action...

Keep thinking about the succession issues facing your organisation right at the top of the agenda. Pylgrim's have already identified that John is not the person to take them through this next phase and that Robert is. Succession is *not* about grey-haired old men waiting to retire.

Note the way in which the combination of people's ideas and the speed of technology can instantly change situations, opportunities, market places and organisations. This energy is transforming places of work and it means that we will need to be constantly assessing who does what in our business.

Identify examples of explicit and tacit knowledge. This may result in highlighting knowledge that is lying dormant or not yet being leveraged for the benefit of your customers.

...so how can action lead to transparency?

Work on developing the tacit knowledge in your organisation through openness and discussion; tacit knowledge lives in people's heads, in relationships, and it thrives in positive cultures. The ability of leaders to use and enhance tacit

How to hit the bull's eye

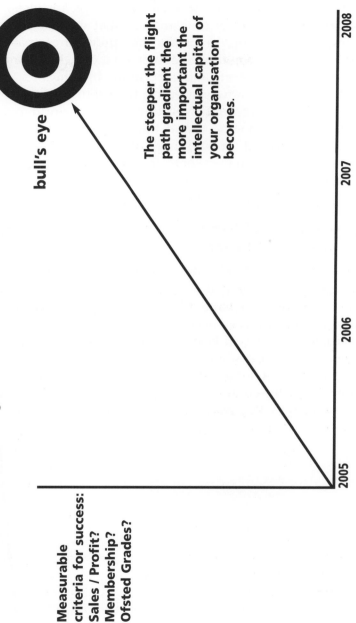

bull's eye

Measurable
criteria for success:
Sales / Profit?
Membership?
Ofsted Grades?

The steeper the flight
path gradient the
more important the
intellectual capital of
your organisation
becomes.

2005

2006

2007

2008

knowledge is vital; this can include feelings, instincts, hunch and experience. Robert now realises that explicit knowledge includes information, processes and procedures that can be copied; it can be stored in a cabinet, on a disc, in a library, in a manual, or on a website and is declining in value.

Pylgrim's have now started on their journey from being a 'dynasty' to a 'dotcom'. Everything in this world is created twice: first we imagine it and then we do it. The bull's eye process is about 'imagining' it. Now Robert has to communicate this to the whole organisation and his team have to do it. By being transparent, there is no way back, providing Robert can develop his vision and keep his nerve.

An example of the TK Factor™ business development process

The chemistry between the founder of a business, the heir apparent and a talented outsider can and often does go one way or another in a matter of seconds. Within a climate of trust, the dynamic process resulting from Robert, John and Ali discussing issues will lead to increased transparency between John and Robert that will help identify what is best for Robert, what is best for John, and most importantly what is best for Pylgrim's in the context of the global knowledge economy. It is this proactivity that leads to the business reward.

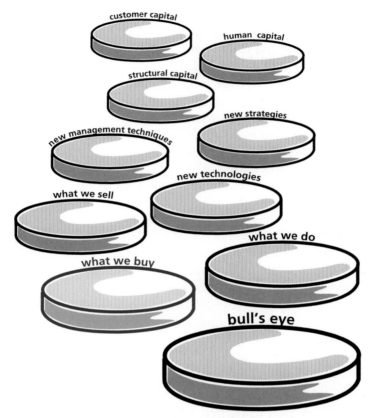

Chapter Two: What We Buy

It was Monday morning. Robert pushed open the door of an office that had changed very little in the last 20 years. Derek Peters glanced up from the letter he was reading and motioned Robert to sit down. It was their weekly meeting, when they discussed the plans for the week ahead and flagged up any potential problems.

"Hello Robert, take a seat. I'll be with you in a moment."

Robert sat down.

"Your father not joining us?"

Robert had to suppress the feeling of irritation those words always engendered. He heard them at least four times a week if not more.

"No, Dad's fishing today."

"Lucky bugger."

Derek had worked with John Pylgrim since the very early days of the business and the men were close friends, although Derek could give John nine years in age.

"Word has it that you've got some consultant in, lad. Is it wise do you think?"

"Wise? What do you mean?"

"Well, happen all they do is create a lot of dust and stir for nought."

"If you mean that he might shake things up here, then I sincerely hope so."

"Eh lad, well I hope you don't live to regret that thought."

"Anyway, you'll get a chance to meet him soon enough. I presume you got my e-mail about the meeting on Friday?"

"Hmmm – we're going to decide on a 'bull's eye', I hear. Some fancy, new-fangled notion is it? Well we managed well enough under your Dad without having to resort to consultants – coming in and telling us what we already know. Bunch of parasites, I reckon."

Robert thought back to his conversation with Ali. "What we buy" – there were certain aspects of Derek that he could quite do without; his outdated notions and dogma being examples. There was no doubt though that no-one knew the production side of the business quite like Derek. And in his day, when they had full manufacturing capacity, he ran the Pylgrim's Porcelain production side like clockwork.

"All this change…I miss the old days you know," Derek commented as if reading Robert's mind. "I miss the hustle and bustle and the smell of the newly baked clay, the stacks of slipware. Nay lad – don't start – I know we had to change – I appreciate that, but it's not the same."

"How's that new designer settling in?" asked Robert, trying to get the meeting back on track.

"He's a bright lad, I'll say that for him, and he's got some wonderful new ideas for a dinner service range – a more modern contemporary feel to it. I have to say I was a bit doubtful about him to begin with – especially the salary you started him on."

"Well he was top of his year at college and we've bought his design capability – that's the future for this business."

"I know and at least he's a local boy – I have to say, I was a bit worried that you might not want to employ locally, you might have ideas about London designers being better."

"Not at all – wherever we can I want to use local people – we'd no choice about buying in from China, we just couldn't compete otherwise, but the staff we have working here I'd like to be from the community as much as possible. We have a duty to a certain extent: corporate responsibility I think they call it. But Josh is going to add real value and enable us to penetrate a new market. We've relied far too long on traditional designs for our tableware."

"I know – we need to catch this new 'upwardly mobile' market."

Robert looked at his notes.

"Has the new consignment come in yet? What's it like?"

"Fair dos to the Chinese, their delivery is spot on and the quality brilliant." Derek sighed, "I can't believe it really – how they do it for the money. Slave labour I suppose."

Robert was indignant, "Indeed it is not! One of the things that took so long when I was over there was checking some of these places out. I know we need to make a profit, but I knew Dad would be horrified if his lifestyle were being supported by the exploitation of some poor Chinese. It does go on, mind you, but there are ethical organisations and the structure of their economy is such that we can still make a healthy saving whilst dealing with a responsible business."

"Well it's amazing to see how our cost base has reduced since we stopped the main manufacture here. I didn't think it was possible when we first started to work like this."

"I'll be over there again soon – perhaps you'd like to come with me and see…"

Robert broke off, as someone knocked hard on the door.

"Come in!"

Josh Lara, the new designer, poked his head round the door.

"Bit of a problem Derek."

"What now?"

"One of those new laser printers has gone funny again."

"Alright lad I'll be right there – technology's great when it works, nuisance when it goes wrong. Some of our old machines just needed a clout with the spanner to get them working again. Quite a knack, though, knowing exactly where to clout it!"

Robert looked up quickly.

"I hope you're not going to wallop that £15k bit of kit with a hammer!"

"Nay lad, fret not! I'll have a look at the program – expect it just needs a slight adjustment."

***

Robert wandered back to his office, musing on time he'd spent with Derek and considering things in the light of his first session with Ali Shah.

They'd invested considerable money in the new technologies to create their new designs and make them compatible with equipment abroad, where the tableware was being made.

The value of explicit knowledge is going down and they were constantly looking for ways to reduce costs where they could. When they downsized they sold off a chunk of land and reinvested the capital in equipment that would put them ahead of the competition.

Robert realised that the reduced value of their tangible assets was a real problem to his father who still had a staunch belief in the value of land, buildings and nice solid, heavy machinery. "Perhaps I need to be a bit more patient with the old boy," he thought.

"Hi Robert," a gangly youth was grinning at him, three steps up on the stairs.

"Hi Josh, how are you settling in?"

"Great thanks, it's a big eye opener working in the real world – I've learnt loads since I've been here."

"Yes we've got some super people in design."

"Yeah, and Derek's amazing – what that guy doesn't know about the industry."

"He's been here a long time."

"But he's so up to date, man. He loves that new printer like a baby! And he's great with customers. It' a real joy watching him do business."

"Well, I'm glad everything's okay. You know my door is always open, so if you have any problems, don't hesitate to come and see me.

***

As Robert opened the door to his office something clicked into place. *Tacit knowledge.* He had bought that when he took Josh on at what Derek considered an exorbitant salary. Instinctively he'd known that at the time. If Pylgrim's Porcelain were to grow, it would be through the quality and freshness of their designs…and designs come out of people's heads.

But talking to Josh had suddenly made him aware of the tacit knowledge under his nose. He'd always thought of Derek as one of the old school, behind the times, always harking on about the good old days. The chat with Josh had made him see Derek with different eyes. Perhaps there was life in the old dog – only time would tell.

***

A week later, Robert was again in Derek's office, but this time there was a marked difference in the atmosphere. Robert felt energised and optimistic – the meeting with Ali had been brilliant – and even Derek was talking with more animation and enthusiasm.

"Fair's fair, that was a bloody good meeting we had. I have to say I really liked your chap – not at all what I expected a consultant to be like – he talked a lot of sense, didn't treat us like a bunch of idiots and managed to get us all working together. And he doesn't mind admitting when he's wrong – thought you were going to sack him at one point!"

Robert was pleased, "So did I, but I felt by the end we'd really achieved something. Even Dad came away feeling we'd finally got a vision for the future. One of the great things about Ali is that he's so passionate about what he does. I feel as if he actually cares about our success, even if he doesn't pull any punches."

"I admit he's not the blood sucking leech I was expecting. You get the impression that he wants to work with us, rather than just tell us what to do and leave us to get on with it."

"It's our bull's eye, though; we agreed it and we signed it off."

Derek laughed, "I thought poor old Malcolm was going to have an apoplexy when Ali put up his balance sheet and suggested that the old fixed assets were no longer the key to primary activity – managing materials and people are not now as important, because customers take process for granted. You can't easily add value through them. Very interesting concept. All credit to the bloke, though, he won Malcolm around eventually."

"And I can see what he means about us starting to think differently – we need to constantly make sure that what we buy is of a high quality. We need to check that the slipware from China is always up to standard and if not, we source elsewhere. Equally, if we are offering personal service, we need to ensure we have staff who can deliver that. We are looking for a different skills set from what we used to have when we made it here."

"I know, like Josh you mean," said Derek.

"Exactly! And that in turn will affect what we do in the business, how we go about making the links with what we buy through to what we sell," added Robert.

"So instead of a factory full of machines, materials and stock on two acres. we have people at computers, on phones and in meetings on one acre."

Robert looked at Derek impressed by his grasp of the issues.

"That's right. So now we have it, the Pylgrim bull's eye! 'We aim to offer exceptional quality products and outstanding personal service for people and organisations that are prepared to pay for collaboration. We will double our turnover from 2 to 4 million in three years' time, with a profit before tax of 15 percent.'"

"You've learnt it off by heart lad?"

"It's *engraved* on my heart Derek"

"It really is about time you got yourself a nice young lady!"

"Give me strength!"

What We Buy: Roadmap for Action

Some people are said to know the cost of everything but the value of nothing and this can become especially apparent when discussing types of intelligence and knowledge. Derek for example, has practical intelligence, Josh specialises in artistic intelligence and Robert appears to have strong emotional intelligence.

The trigger experience...

At a recent board meeting, one director was advising colleagues that a crucial piece of land had not been purchased because he 'was not getting on too well', with the two vendors, whom he had in fact known for years. He added that he resented 'paying the premium the vendors were asking, which is 50 percent more than the market value of the land'. The board could be given no date for the purchase, because he had 'handed the project to property agents'.

Their adviser replied that even without the figures, his *instinct* said that the adjacent land was an essential purchase rather than cheaper piecemeal plots making up the same area in various remote locations. His *feeling* was that the director should pick up the phone and take the vendors out for a drink to do the deal, even at a premium.

The director completed the deal the next day, at half the original premium that had been asked. This highly successful outcome for the director, the company (and the adviser) is an example of how *tacit knowledge* works.

Note that the trigger experience for Robert is the recognition of Derek's tacit knowledge and the catalyst was new boy Josh....

...this experience leads to thoughts...

Look at each and every employee from the perspective of how to identify, enhance and then leverage their knowledge for the benefit of the business. Don't dismiss, take for granted or be unaware of some of the valuable knowledge in a Pylgrim's type business such as that possessed by Derek.

Identify the intellectual capital in your organisation starting with what you buy. When you buy something, whether it is purchasing a camera, a car, software or someone's skill, it is highly probable that it will contain more knowledge than a similar purchase made in the recent past. People, for example, are becoming more knowledgeable, more flexible and more mobile than ever before.

Recognise that activities such as buying it, making it and selling it are the very minimum competences that customers expect today.

Take a look now at 'Everyone is good at something' on the opposite page. The middle cloud contains three types of intelligence that are going to become more and more important in the global economy. Some types of intelligence are more valuable to some organisations than they are to others; Josh, for example, may not be so effective working in a firm of solicitors.

Start to think of everything that you buy for the business in terms of whether it will eventually either reduce costs or add value for your customers.

...thoughts lead to decisions and action...

Attract the very best people you can afford, and then keep and develop them. Either you can employ winners from the start, which is very expensive, or you can employ potential winners. The most helpful paradigm of managing people is that everyone on the payroll is potentially a winner, including Derek.

Emphasise activities such as research and development; marketing strategy, training and customer relationships, the very things that were once regarded as support activities.

Everyone is good at something

Factual
That 'know-it-all' knowledge of the encyclopaedia.

Analytical
The ability to reason and conceptualise.

Numerate
Being at ease with numbers of all sorts.

A combination of these first three intelligences will get you through most examinations and entitle you to be called 'clever'.
But there is more to intelligence than this.

A narrow focus on the first three intelligences, runs the risk of labelling as stupid those who do not shine in those particular arenas. But they may have great skills in other areas.

Intuitive
An aptitude for sensing and seeing what is not immediately obvious.

Emotional
An awareness of others, self-awareness and self control.

Interpersonal
The ability to get things done with and through others.

Linguistic
A facility with language.

Spatial
An ability to see patterns.

Athletic
Some might call this talent.

Practical
Often called common sense!

Realising everyone's intelligence is part of developing the intellectual capital of an organisation.

Outsource your manufacturing to China and it may create a competitive advantage for a time, but only until a competitor does the same. Buying Chinese labour is an 'explicit knowledge' act.

Reduce costs through sourcing cheaper explicit knowledge whilst at the same time adding value for customers by increasing high-value tacit knowledge. Research suggests that we pay more for potential knowledge workers but that they add more long-term added value than cheaper unskilled workers.

Sort out your intangible assets such as people on the payroll, patents, copyrights and customer relations from the tangible assets such as land and buildings, plant and machinery. Then start to grow the intangible to tangible ratio faster than your competitors.

...so how can action lead to transparency?

When working towards a bull's eye everyone starts to use language more congruently. Since the answer to the first bull's eye question for Pylgrim's (What do we want to be?) is to be 'offering exceptional quality products and outstanding personal service' then their performance, the delivery of their core competencies to customers, is forced to match the words. In other words, we must do what we say we do.

An example of the TK Factor™ business development process

The combination of all the tacit knowledge within the senior management team (SMT) has resulted in a bull's eye that everyone has bought into and collectively signed off. Individuals have become more transparent through the process; they have shared goals, values, feelings and ideas in order to create a vision for the future. The bull's eye has initiated a framework and common language that enhances understanding and the reward is to clarify everyone's role in the future success of Pylgrim's.

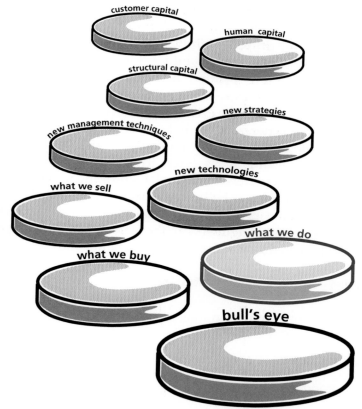

customer capital

human capital

structural capital

new strategies

new management techniques

new technologies

what we sell

what we do

what we buy

bull's eye

Chapter Three: What We Do

"OK, I think it's time we got down to business." Robert gazed around the table and the chatter gradually subsided.

"Let's start with this month's figures. Malcolm, how are things looking budget to actual?"

Malcolm, the accountant, 55, greying, ex-rugby player running a little to fat, shuffled his papers and looked round at the assembled company, Derek on his right, John to his left, and Ruth and Robert opposite. He picked up a pile of papers and started to hand them around.

"As you can see the figures for this month are pretty much

on target. That pilot order from Terrisons has helped and cash flow is looking healthy."

Robert's mind drifted slightly as Malcolm with his usual pedantic style started to go into some detail. Robert was interested in the big picture; he found the minutiae less interesting but made some effort to overcome this in his new role as MD. He was aware that he needed to cope with all aspects of the business and he knew that his poor attention to detail frustrated Malcolm. As indeed Robert's perception of Malcolm's nit-picking ways often irritated him. But Robert knew it was down to him to try harder. His mind snapped back to attention, however, as he heard Malcolm comment:

"I do have some grave concerns, however, when we come to compare this month's figures with those for this time last year."

Robert looked down at the sheet in his hand, and focused his mind.

"Sales are up Malcolm," but he knew what was coming, "The bull's eye..."

"Sales are one thing, but look at our expenditure!"

"This is about our investment programme – you know that."

Robert could feel the tension rising. John peered over his glasses.

"No good hitting our bull's eye if we don't make a profit, son."

"Exactly John, knew you'd see it my way."

Malcolm's grin was smug.

"Not saying that Malcolm," John glared at him.

"We're changing how we do things," said Robert. "At this stage it costs, but the bull's eye is about profit."

"And gross profit is only 5 percent behind last year." Support came from an unexpected quarter and Derek continued, "And sales seem to be creeping up month on month," he rustled through the papers in his hand, "As is the net profit." He looked around the room. "I have to confess when we set the bull's eye as doubling our turnover in three years I was a bit sceptical. In fact both you and I John were against it to begin with. It took quite some um, er...discussion...to convince us that it was a viable proposition. But I can see that with this Terrisons' order, and Robert's plans for changing what we do, that it is not the pie in the sky I originally thought."

Malcolm was keen to get back to making his point.

"Yes, yes, okay. But profits would be better if we reduced some of this high expenditure. Look at these new paints and glazes you're buying, they're much more expensive than the old ones we used to get."

"With all these various initiatives and legislation coming in, we need to be very aware of our effect on the environment. These new paints have much better pigments, they don't pollute and many of them are coming from sustainable resources."

"You're just naïve Robert. No good being a tree-hugging fluffy bunny if we go out of business because we can't make a profit!"

Malcolm's voice was starting to rise.

"And it's no good screwing down our costs if we're then closed down as a hazard to the environment or because we're not compliant with legislation," Robert's tone was cool.

Malcolm changed tack, "Well, look at this new lad, Josh Lara. His salary is twice what you were paying some of the old staff – the ones you had to get rid of when you were cutting back."

His tone took on a bitter quality. An uncomfortable silence filled the room, a vacuum into which everyone was reluctant to speak.

"But Josh's talent is probably worth two of some of those people," Robert eventually commented.

"What exactly are you implying?" Malcolm started to get to his feet. "Are you saying that Irene has got no talent?"

"No one is saying that," interjected Ruth calmingly, soothingly.

"Of course not Malcolm, we were very sorry that we had to

let Irene go, any of them go, but we'd no choice, you know that."

John looked uncomfortable as he always did when the topic of the 30 redundancies came up.

"Come on Malcolm, sit down, have some more coffee."

Ruth had come round the table and was filling his cup; whilst at the same time placing a placatory hand on his shoulder, pressing him gently down into his seat.

"I saw Irene last week in town," she continued. "She seems to love her new job."

"Yes well, that's as maybe, but it's not the point," Malcolm went on. "I still think that we could cut costs, get someone cheaper than this Josh – we've never paid the designers as much as we pay him."

"But the design is everything now," said Derek, "and the kid is a bloody marvel. I'll give him his due, he always seems to know what people want – especially the new market that we're going for."

He tapped the sheet in front of him.

"This Terrisons' order – it's all the new contemporary stuff that they want."

"He's right Malcolm," added Robert. "We have to do things differently now and the bill for the designers has gone up because that's what we have to do now."

"But the whole point of getting it made in China was to reduce our costs!"

"And to make us more efficient. In fact one of the things I wanted to raise today was our plans for bringing on another designer as well as some ideas Ali Shah and I have been discussing…"

"And that's another thing," Malcolm was getting heated again. "I've seen his invoice for that day we did. What on earth are we paying this man a king's ransom for? OK I admit it was useful, but we could get rid of him now. That in itself would cut our expenditure considerably. I'm still amazed that you agreed to this, John. Consultants! How often have I heard you say that you wouldn't give them the time of day?"

"Not this again!" Robert slumped back in his chair.

"Well perhaps I did, but the world's changing and changing fast. Not sure I understand how business works anymore. Time was when we made our bits and pieces and customers phoned up to order."

For a moment he looked old and defeated; then he straightened his back and continued briskly. "Happen he's come up with some good ideas though, I'll give him that. And the bull's eye has helped clarify a focus for the business; I can see more of a future, which I have to say I've been finding hard to do over the last few years. And Derek's right, I did need some convincing that doubling turnover was possible, especially when you consider how we have struggled recently. But at least this Ali chap is helping us to see *how* we can do it."

"Yes, well it was OK I suppose, but as you know, I was very dubious that we were talking more in terms of turnover and less about profit."

"But it's not just about profit. You know that and you signed it off with the rest of us!" exclaimed Robert, "You can't renege on that now!"

"And I have to add Malcolm" said John, "that I have *never* run this business purely for profit. I've loved every bit of this factory and the people who have worked here. Yes, okay, I'll admit making money is not something I'm averse to but I could have screwed far more out of it if all I'd wanted was the biggest dividend I could get!"

"And anyway," added Robert, "profit will come later when we've invested the money into finding cust…"

"Well that's all well and good, but, I'm not sure we'll ever find the sort of customers…"

Malcolm did not finish as Robert leaned forward excitedly, "Actually I've been thinking about that. This could be an opportunity to move into the bespoke hand-painted market!"

"But we got rid of all the painters when we bought the new equipment. I thought that labour-intensive work was the last road we want to be going down – correct me if I'm wrong!" Malcolm exclaimed.

"Labour intensive becomes knowledge intensive when you can command the price – we couldn't before," Robert continued. "The beauty of this idea is that we would be aiming at the very high end of the market!"

"And does this fit in with the bull's eye?" Malcolm smiled.

"Of course it does, this is about personal service; we'd be working closely with our customers to produce bespoke items, very expensive. There's a place in London that sells this service to their clients and we're talking upmarket. Whole dinner services hand designed and painted to specific customer requirements, you know, each plate, bowl and cup with 'V' and 'D' entwined in gold leaf."

"V and D?"

"Victoria and David."

"Who?"

"Beckham!"

"Oh, right."

"Anyway, this is just an idea at the moment but I'm going to do some market research and some networking – make a few contacts. Ali has recommended a really good market research company…"

"I don't believe it! More expense! And what'll we have to show for it exactly?"

"A whole new marketing strategy for a start!"

"Marketing strategy?" Malcolm seemed to struggle to find the words. "It's all so, so…nebulous! When we used to buy things, we bought *things*, now we seem to be buying 'ideas' or 'talent' or 'software' or 'technology' or a 'strategy', but we no longer have anything concrete to get hold of. Even the stuff we import from China is never here very long, it's all 'just in time' and instant communication. I used to love walking through the warehouse looking at the piles of stock." He ran a hand distractedly through his hair. "We just don't do what we did."

"Do what you've always done and you'll get what you've

always got. If we'd carried on like that we'd have gone bust."
Ruth spoke quietly but with authority. "Look, Ali may be pricey
but if he helps this company through a period of change, then
he'll have been worth his weight in gold."

John looked at this watch. "She's right, you know, come on,
time we were cracking on. Now then, next on the agenda…"

***

Two days later, Robert was sitting with Ali in his office.

"I feel sometimes not so much that we're on a flight path
toward the bull's eye, but that I am dragging them kicking and
screaming to it! Some of the meetings we're having seem to be
so acrimonious; we seem to be having arguments all the time at
the moment."

"Trust me Robert, it'll get better. You've been used to a way
of doing things that encouraged the status quo. Heads down;
people doing their own thing. But everything you now do is
becoming much more transparent and people can no longer
hide behind outmoded practices. This is bound to cause
arguments in the first instance. You're just unused to dealing
with conflict, but you'll get much, much better at it."

"But surely we want to avoid conflict, that can't be a good
thing if we are always rowing?"

"They fight, you argue, I engage in robust discussion!
Conflict is a hugely positive thing if it is handled right. If there
were no conflict there'd be stagnation; conflict is what moves
things forward. Good quality relationships are ones where
we're open about ourselves, where others are open in their
feedback to us and where we learn more about ourselves as a
consequence. This comes through dialogue and discussion and
does not shy away from talking about issues that have to be
addressed."

"So will I win Malcolm around eventually?"

"I can't guarantee that, but what I will say is that what you
do and how you do it – the way your people interact with each
other, with your stakeholders, with your customers and adapt

to the speed of change – will be crucial to your success. And the culture you are creating will either draw people like magnets or repel them. There'll be natural fall-out as a consequence, but once you've set your stall out you'll find like-minded people who'll really want to succeed with you; people who actually get really excited about the prospect!"

"You mean I'll be able to attract all those potential winners out there."

"Exactly! It really is a pleasure to work with you, you know!"

Robert looked surprised.

"Oh?"

"Yes, you are eager to learn, willing to try something new and to stay with the pain. I really admire that."

"But don't all your clients? Why pay for your advice if you are not going to act on it?

Ali laughed.

What We Do: Roadmap for Action

If what we buy is gradually, inevitably, containing more and more knowledge, then what we actually do at work is also going to have to change. Old habits, maybe habits of a lifetime, may no longer be appropriate in the context of the bull's eye for the business. Malcolm in particular seems to be having problems in adjusting to the newer, more robust regime that is resulting from Robert gradually taking control from his father, John.

The trigger experience...

One long-established UK family business specialises in dress hire. It has several distinct income streams but because of changes in the market place, competitor activity and rapidly changing customer needs it is in trouble.

The managing director had been in post for 20 years and he cannot understand why a business that has been successful for three generations should not respond to all the old ways of working. In exasperation, he slams his fist on the desk and exclaims, 'What do you do when the phone stops ringing?'

And there is the answer to the problem. In the global knowledge economy, you never wait for the phone to stop ringing – for that is a reactive paradigm. You have to constantly be looking for new contacts, new opportunities, new ways of working. You have to be proactive to be a winner.

See how Robert is really up against it to change the mindset of some of his older, more experienced colleagues. This is a battle that *has* to be won if Pylgrim's are going to be winners.

Note that John is starting to question the business beliefs that he has deployed successfully for so many years: the trigger experience for him was halving his workforce. The old models worked when there were tariffs, quotas, demand exceeded supply, and customer care as a concept had not been invented! A proactive approach requires people to go out and find the business through networking strategies, e-marketing or new product/service launches.

...this experience leads to thoughts...

Realise that the older the average age of a board of directors, the harder it is for them to really take on board new skills, new knowledge and new attitudes, yet that is precisely what is required. Watch out for people who pay lip service to change but actually carry on behaving in the same old ways; there may be a limit to what the old team will be able to do differently.

Be aware of the need to constantly examine new ways of doing things and new ways of working. For example, assess 'unskilled, labour-intensive' businesses where the only route to competitive advantage is by reducing the cost of labour. This means relocating elements of production to lower-cost economies in other parts of the world or using immigrant labour at home.

Apply the same principle to 'material-intensive' businesses. As distribution networks consolidate and goods are manufactured more cheaply overseas, gross margins to be made on buying goods for resale is in decline. Consider entirely new income streams with your existing customer base by increasing the offer of tacit in proportion to explicit knowledge!

Note that 'machine intensive' businesses can create a competitive advantage with their high-tech design or process capability, just as long as a competitor does not have the same one. In the global knowledge economy, where more and more of our competencies are becoming transparent via the net (particularly explicit, copyable ones), that advantage may not last as long as the famous 'Marks and Spencer prawn sandwich'.

Look for simplicity in what people do since as the world becomes more complex, simplicity is becoming more valuable. Organisations must be on their guard against getting bogged down by complexity; by other people's problems and by wasting time not dealing with the jugular issues.

Recognise that employees will specialise in areas of knowledge that we know little or nothing about. Manage and leverage this knowledge in the most effective and straightforward way possible. The beauty of Robert's idea to leverage existing tacit knowledge to offer hand-painted designs is its simplicity.

...thoughts lead to decisions and action...

Aspire to being a 'knowledge-intensive' organisation, since it is through unique tacit knowledge that we can successfully differentiate ourselves from our competitors. Knowledge-intensive businesses can generate the highest earnings per employee. Robert's idea of suggesting a bespoke service, if it is done right and reaches the correct market, could be a successful new income stream.

Seek out the much closer links between what we buy, what we do and what we sell that are apparent today. One view round the table at Pylgrim's is that Josh, the new young designer, is overpaid. However, they brought Josh in to change what they do and to change what they sell.

Work at improving the quality of all relationships within the organisation. How people work with and respond to each other is vital. Don't fear healthy conflict, but work with it. Ensure issues are resolved and that respect is maintained even when differences of opinion occur.

The bull's eye process often means we need to look for new, bigger or better quality customers, those that are prepared to pay for a bespoke business relationship. Pylgrim's may want to look at replicating the relationship they have with Terrisons, for example. This in turn can mean repositioning or a change in marketing strategy.

Plan to change in order to grow

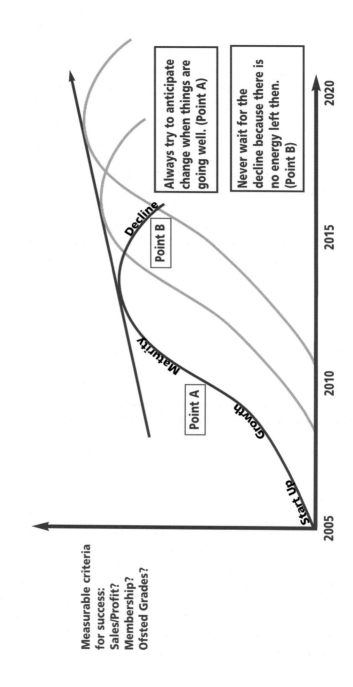

50

Use the Sigmoid curve (see 'Plan to change in order to grow' on the opposite page) to change the way people think in your organisation. This model depicts the life cycle of businesses, relationships, governments and even empires. There is the start-up phase, growth, maturity and inevitable decline. And if that were all there was to the model, pretty depressing it would be. However, the good news is that, as time passes, it is possible to create a new curve, and then another. Each successive curve is designed to replace or enhance the previous one.

Deploy resources to do this work at the growth phase on the original curve. At this stage, people are optimistic and positive because things are going well. Unfortunately, many leave the work on the new curve until the decline phase on the original curve, when people are not sufficiently resourceful, energised or enthusiastic. Then it is too late!

...so how can action lead to transparency?

Add value for customers today by being right up to speed on what your competitors are doing, fully aware of what your customers really want and absolutely on top of what is happening in the market place. These three external factors are all outside your organisation, yet they can have an exponential impact on what the business does on the inside.

An example of the TK Factor™ business development process:

At the SMT meeting, Malcolm in particular has a series of issues he feels strongly about. There is nothing wrong with conflict; it is a healthy ingredient of many winning teams. However, an atmosphere of hostility or adversarialism has to be dealt with fast. With Ali's help, Robert is beginning to tap into his own tacit knowledge that he is gaining confidence in using. Robert has a new idea for developing a bespoke range, which he shares with the SMT. Ideally John's experience, Derek's knowledge, Malcolm's scepticism and eventually Josh's talent can combine to reward the company with a potential new income stream.

51

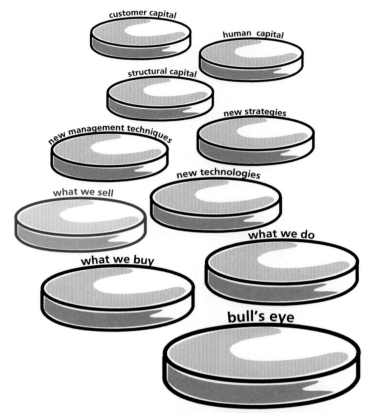

Chapter Four: What We Sell

"Hello, Robert – can you pop down for a minute?" Derek's voice boomed down the telephone.

"Can't it wait, Derek? I've got a stack of paperwork to finish." Robert glanced at his watch. "And it's ten to five, Derek – you know I'm trying to break you from your long hours mentality. Work–life balance and all that."

"Hmmm – you young ones today don't know what work is – when I were an apprentice I didn't think twice about working 10 hours a day – and none of this nonsense about regular breaks. When the machines were going right we made the most of it!"

Robert grinned, "You're still sore because that health and safety chap called you a dinosaur."

"And what you really want to do lad, is get on the golf course in half an hour."

"What? That's not fair, I've done..."

"Only joking – I know the hours you've put in getting this place to rights. Just give us half an hour – it is important."

"Alright – I'll be down in 10 minutes."

***

At least, Robert reflected, things had improved. Six months ago, Derek wouldn't have rung up; he'd have just 'dropped in', a habit Robert was trying to break the whole workforce from, as it played havoc with their time management.

Fifteen minutes later Robert was in Derek's office staring into the mug of tea he had just been handed.

"Do I drink this, or creosote the fence with it?" he asked.

"It'll put hairs on your chest, lad – get it down you. Now then, we've got a bit of a problem."

"Oh?"

"Terrisons – the supermarket people."

"They've not cancelled their order?"

"No, nothing like that – Gerald's been in to see them today." Gerald Seymour was Pylgrim's salesman, "And the fact is they are so pleased with the stuff they've had from us, they'd like us to design a new range for them called 'The Garden Range' – but more traditional in style!"

"But that's excellent!" exclaimed Robert.

"We just can't do it – I've got the designers working flat out at the moment, even wonder boy Josh. We're just not geared up for this – they want to collaborate with us as it's to fit in with their summer outdoor living feature they want to do in a couple of months' time. I think we're going to have to turn them down."

"We can't turn them down – this is *just* the sort of work we need!"

"I don't think they are going to want to pay over the odds, though – they'll want a nice tight price, not far adrift from what they're paying for the off-the-peg range. Want to save their money for some poncey TV designer they're going to use to promote 'Alfresco Living' – whatever that is!"

"Then we'll just have to find a way of giving them the service they want in the timescale at the right price. If we can really sell them the added value we can offer, then we may be able to negotiate the price."

"But that doesn't solve the problem of how we are to fit this in. The amount of input they want to have means we'll need someone dedicated to this work for two or three months – I just can't do it."

"Leave it with me for a bit," said Robert, "When have you promised to get back to them by?"

"Couple of days."

"OK, I'll have a chat with Dad and see if we can come up with anything. My gut instinct is that we have to do this."

"Just tell me how and I'll be right behind you."

***

Robert thought back to his conversation with Ali Shah a few days ago. He thought about the concept of service and all the routes to competitive advantage, such as their research and development capability, reducing labour costs. They had managed to halve the workforce and despite Malcolm's consternation about Josh's salary, their labour costs were down through using their Chinese manufacturers.

Next day, Robert was in his father's office discussing the Terrisons dilemma with him.

"We've got to do this, Robert, if we don't we may be in danger of losing all the Terrisons' business!"

"I know, Dad, but how? We haven't got time to take on and train someone new, and besides, it's only a project for a couple of months. It might develop into something bigger, but at present we can't make a case for more staff. Malcolm would hit the roof!"

John looked up from the paper on which he was doodling elaborate designs.

"Perhaps you could do it, Dad?" joked Robert.

"No son, too busy working on getting my handicap down."

"I'll believe that when you are actually out of this place for longer than one day a week!"

John ignored him. "But I do have an idea. More traditional design did you say they wanted?"

"Yes, flowers, plants and things."

"Well what about Irene?"

"Irene's got a job."

"Not any more she hasn't – her elderly mum has come to live with them and she needs more care than Irene can give her and go out to work."

"Sorry, you've lost me Dad."

"Don't you ever listen to that Ali chap? The amount we're paying him you should be etching his words indelibly in your head!"

"Dad, of course I listen!" Robert held up his hand. "No Dad, please don't quote that old comment of Mrs Johnson's on my school report – I was only eight at the time!"

"Ha! I'd forgotten about her!" John laughed. "That woman scared the living daylights out of me, let alone all the little beggars in her class. I remember one parents' evening…"

"Dad! Please keep to the point!" At least, Robert thought to himself, his father's reminiscences only had him as an audience this time. It was not unknown even now for his father to embarrass him in front of the staff with some family recollection or schoolboy misdemeanour – which did nothing for Robert's credibility or self-esteem.

"Irene?" asked Robert.

"Yes son. She could do this work for us from home. We could use her on a temporary contract basis for the duration of this project. Outsourcing some of the extra design work we get in could be a real option for us in the future. What did Ali say – something about the increasing need for flexible working practices? The beauty also is that floral designs were always Irene's strong suit. We can get the transfers made up and it will be easy enough to get them put onto the whiteware."

"But what about communicating with Terrisons? She is going to have to be in touch with them on a regular basis – sending designs and tweaking them!"

"What's the point of having a computer whiz kid in the family and not using her?"

"What, Kate?" asked Robert, "I'm not sure she'll have the time or the energy," he said, thinking of his sister, now eight months pregnant and just about to go on maternity leave.

"Of course she will – I spoke to her last night and she's bloody annoyed her doctor insists she finishes a month before her due date."

"Well Dad, with respect, the amount of travelling she has to do..."

"I know all that, but the point is that she has no desire to sit and twiddle her thumbs for a month. A bit of gentle work here's just what she wants."

Robert looked at his father, "This all sounds a little bit too convenient, Dad, I have to say."

His father looked sheepish, "Okay, I will admit that I have been looking for an opportunity to try and give Kate a bit to do. I've always felt bad about never having offered her..."

"And what about Irene; just feeling sorry for her as well?"

His father looked pleased, "Now that was pure inspiration, son, honestly. You'd call it thinking outside the box I expect! She really would be ideal – good design skills, always got on well with customers, great with computers. We only made her redundant because at that time we couldn't use her in the old way we were working. But as you keep telling me we are doing things differently now!"

Robert started to catch some of his father's excitement. "So Kate can set up a system that allows Irene to communicate with us online and with the client. We can even lend Irene some hardware and the software she needs."

"Whatever… I'll leave the computer speak to you. And I'm sure she'll be able to come and work here occasionally as long as she doesn't leave her mum for too long. What do you reckon?"

Robert watched the animation in his father's face and listened to the passion in his voice. Really the old boy never ceased to surprise him. Robert caught a glimmer of his father's old self – and something beyond that – the vigour and enthusiasm that set the business up originally, before it grew to the proportions where his father was forced to stop doing the things he loved and had to do all the things he hated. Robert felt a twinge of envy. If his father was a born creator – was he, Robert, a born manager? And how sad was that? He'd have to run that one past Ali Shah.

***

He had the opportunity a couple of days later.

"There are two issues here," explained Ali. "Following on from what we're talking about in terms of 'what we do' you are the ideal person to manage that process, precisely because you have the skills *to* manage. Much of what we've been talking about over the last few months requires a helicopter vision which I'm delighted to say you have – otherwise I might have been forced to sack you."

"What…?"

"I jest Robert," Ali's rather dry sense of humour often put Robert on a back foot.

"However, you're quite correct in thinking that your father's creativity and indeed the creativity of your team as a whole is pretty crucial in terms of what you sell. You intend to sell Irene's creativity to Terrisons; you're selling the uniqueness of Josh's designs already, which is brilliant. It is about customisation. Did you know you can go online and have a pair of trainers made to your own specification?"

"Whatever next! But you're right, Ali, Irene is bloody good, you know. We always seem to go on about Josh and his ability, but Irene has an exquisite and delicate way with colour and pattern. I'm sure she will be able to do just what Terrisons want."

"But you must not underestimate the value of the other things you are selling, which come mainly from your own unique ability."

"Do you mean service?" asked Robert. "Don't want to blow my own trumpet, but I suppose that with all these creative types around it would be very easy to get caught up in the creative process and never deliver. I try to keep them all on track and make sure we are providing the turnaround times and deadlines our customers want."

"Exactly. But it is much more than that, you know, it is about your leadership. Your energy, your enthusiasm, your total commitment to fulfilling customer expectations not only communicates itself to your staff, who, I think, would follow you through fire and brimstone, but also transmits itself to your clients and that is an enormous asset."

"You mean people buy people?" asked Robert.

"A bit trite possibly, but yes. You have an intuitive connection with your customers, which is invaluable. Don't underestimate it!"

"Well thanks Ali, it's nice of you to say that. I do feel better."

"Please don't misunderstand me. I don't say anything to be 'nice' and rest assured when it is time to kick arse, I'll do so!"

"So you weren't joking earlier were you?"

"How do you mean?"

"You bloody well would've sacked me if I hadn't been up to scratch."

Ali just smiled.

What We Sell: Roadmap for Action

When we do things differently, it should result in either adding value for customers or reducing costs; these are the two routes towards competitive advantage. At Pylgrim's there is an immediate challenge from an important new customer, Terrisons, not only to do things differently, but to sell an entirely new service. By tapping into the unique tacit knowledge of Irene's design and Kate's IT specialisms, there is the opportunity to collaborate on a brand new project.

The trigger experience...

One large UK accountancy client can see very little future in some of the taxation and audit activities that were the mainstay of their business for so many years. They are having to revisit their business model in order to see whether traditional income streams are still valid for the future.

When they received a call from India offering to complete jobs for less than half the cost they would pay in the UK, they realised the extent of overseas competition. But the real problem is the nature of the work. It involves compliance; it involves the use of explicit knowledge that is simply less valuable today.

So get used to seeing less signs saying 'Chartered Accountants' and many more from the same people being described as 'Business advisers and consultants'.

What about the conversation between John and Robert as a trigger experience? John is solving Robert's problem using his own ability to think differently.

...this experience leads to thoughts...

Realise that some people have an auditory learning style preference, some a visual and some a tactile learning style preference. This knowledge can change the way we sell as we try to hook into the learning preferences of our customers. Irene probably has a visual learning style preference herself, but she may have to find other ways to tap into the understanding of her client.

Be aware that research suggests that the left-hand side of our brain is about lists, logic, numbers and sequence whereas the right-hand side is about colours, imagination, ideas and creativity. We need to consider both sides when presenting to customers. It's the words that are used to convey both Josh's designs and Irene's colours that are an important part of selling today.

Improve your offering to your customers by considering how to multi-skill. Some engineering companies, for example, are recognising that traditional sales force approaches are not as successful as getting engineers off the benches and out to work in *collaboration* with customers. They then link these site meetings online back to colleagues at base.

Genuine openness, honesty and transparency is extremely demanding and websites encourage this. The same rules, however, apply to our competitors, so stay right up to speed with what they are offering to your customers and react accordingly.

...thoughts lead to decisions and action...

Decide on your new income streams but make sure they are something customers want, something competitors cannot easily copy and remember to attach a meter (the profit and cash forecast!). If you go into the market simply to buy knowledge, competitors can do the same.

Increase the knowledge intensity of your products and services by adding more value where possible. A 'knowledge idea' itself does not necessarily have to be high tech; it could be a superior credit control system; it could be cutting the time to do a job from three hours to two. At Pylgrim's it is about employing Irene in a different way and exploiting her talent.

Make sure that everyone is able to sell themselves, new products and services and your organisation. Robert must transmit his enthusiasm and his sense of direction to everyone materially involved with Pylgrim's. He can help anyone to become measurably better in this absolutely vital life skill – that is, selling.

Break down the silo mentality, the old adversarial conflicts between, say, sales and production, that was so common in the 'old' economy. You cannot have any department or function thinking or behaving as if it is superior to another. All internal relationships exist to serve the customer. So Kate and Irene will have to find ways of working together. See the model 'An imperative need for greater creativity' on page 64.

Learning developments in your organisation will only happen with the right culture and culture *always* comes from the top. Just listening to the way that John and Robert are discussing the Terrisons project is an example of how people can change the way they think about themselves and their business. When we think differently about something, then we can change what we actually do. When we change what we do, we can improve what we sell.

...so how can action lead to transparency?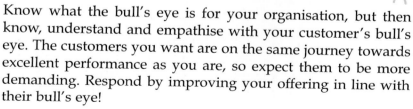

Know what the bull's eye is for your organisation, but then know, understand and empathise with your customer's bull's eye. The customers you want are on the same journey towards excellent performance as you are, so expect them to be more demanding. Respond by improving your offering in line with their bull's eye!

An imperative need for greater creativity

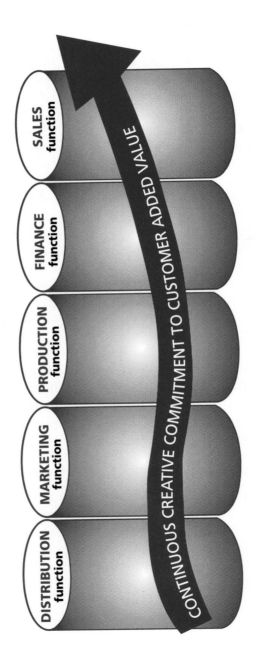

A creative and innovative culture stems from everyone striving to fulfil their potential in the context of the organisation, whatever the function, whatever their job.

An example of the TK Factor™ business development process:

Robert has encouraged Derek to use his tacit knowledge in the relationship with Terrisons, who want Pylgrim's to develop a new range. Robert explores his father's knowledge and experience; he rightly looks to him for a solution to the dilemma of how to resource the project. There are several lateral solutions used: both Kate and Irene are to be brought in and the project will require complete transparency with Terrisons. This sort of thinking – the synergy between people – can be so rewarding in developing collaboration and enhanced customer relationships.

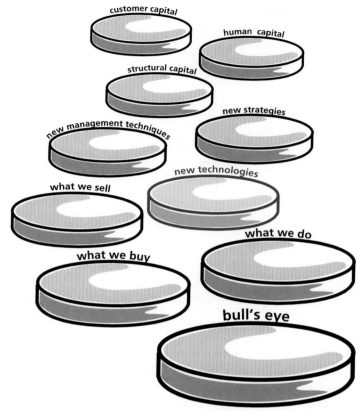

Chapter Five: New Technologies

Kate sat back in her chair, adjusted the cushion behind her back and gave her brother a level look.

"Well, aren't I honoured?" she said

Robert looked at her.

"What's that supposed to mean?"

"Well, I've not been asked to contribute anything to the family business since I was 16 years old, just done my GCSEs and was allowed to sweep the factory floor for two months."

"But you've never wanted to..."

"I was never asked!"

"Look Kate, I'm sorry if…"

Kate sighed and shifted into a more comfortable position.

"Don't worry, Robert, I'm not really annoyed – I'm very happy with the opportunities we had and the choices I've made."

She grinned at her brother.

"Just couldn't resist having a bit of a dig – I do get arsy at everyone's assumption that it would be you who followed in Dad's footsteps. Boy, eldest, all that crap."

Robert looked at his sister, thought of a hundred and one things he might say, but knew deep down that she was probably right.

"Dad's just a bit old fashioned…but in fairness it was his idea to bring you in now."

"Not your choice you mean."

"Honestly, Kate, I…"

"Look, let's just forget it shall we? You're lucky I'm extremely fond of you otherwise we might have some real family conflict."

Robert returned her smile.

"Perhaps it was fortunate you weren't the elder – then Dad would have had a really tough decision between primogeniture and inheritance through the male line."

There were only a couple of years in age between the two of them and they had been close as children. Less so as they grew older and went their separate ways, but there was a deep-rooted fondness and respect for each other that re-surfaced whenever they met up.

"So do you think you could help? What's your doctor say?"

"He's fine, it was the travel he was concerned about. A bit of office work here or from home won't be a problem."

"That's great! To be honest I don't know why Dad's not asked you in before to look at the computer system."

"Well, in fairness, when I finished my degree and was looking for a job, Pylgrim's was about 20 years behind the times as far as technology was concerned! It's only really in the last five years with you coming on board that things have progressed so much. By the time I could have been of use, I was already working my butt off at Laurel UK. And anyway, even saying that, you're not exactly Mr Proactive in terms of buying technology!"

"What!"

"Oh come on Robert, you have to admit it!"

"But we are really up to date with technology."

"You're up to date – but you've done it so piecemeal and every time you get a new bit of equipment you often have to change other bits. You've got no long-term strategy and your system needs a complete overhaul. It's not just about what you need today – it's about what you are going to need tomorrow."

"But you can't really know what you're going to need tomorrow!"

Kate grinned: "You can if you ask an expert like me!"

"You're enjoying this, aren't you, little sister?"

"You bet!" Kate laughed. "And not so much of the 'little'!" Kate patted her stomach.

***

Two days later Robert and John were having a chat.

"That sister of yours is going to cost me an arm and a leg with her 'shopping list' as she calls it!"

"That daughter of yours is having a whale of a time, and I must say, adding real value."

"Hmm – well I'm going to have to trust you on that – as you know, my computer skills are somewhat limited."

"The key thing she's done is to take a helicopter view of our whole system, so that we can not only integrate a lot of our processes better, but also work much more efficiently. She's linked Irene up so that she can scan her designs and transmit them online to Terrisons. The video conferencing set up she wants to organise here will mean that Irene and I will be able to discuss the designs with our contact at Terrisons and the designer who is going to 'brand it' for them."

"But why does she want all this new stuff, son? I can see where we could be buying new bits we've not had before, but why replace items that we've got that seem to be working perfectly well?"

As Robert opened his mouth to answer, the door opened and Kate herself entered.

"Is this a private meeting or can anyone join in?"

"Kate, Dad was just wondering…"

"I know, I heard him – why you couldn't discuss this with me, Dad, rather than Robert, I don't know. No wonder Mum chose never to work here."

John winced.

"Your Mum thought bringing you two up was far more important than going out to work."

"If this is a dig because I intend to return to work after this sprog is born, then…"

Robert sighed. Why did they always have to antagonise each other? Kate knew that Dad still found it painful to talk about the death of their mum two years earlier. Yet Kate had to mention her. And as for Dad…

"Alright you two, enough – this is business we are supposed to be discussing. Kate, please tell Dad your reasons for replacing some of our existing equipment."

Kate looked at her brother, decided not to say what she was going to say and enveloped herself in professional authority.

"It's about scaleability. Your whole system needs to be able to grow without fundamental structural change. By tweaking your present system now, we'll be able to do that."

"What about all this training? Looks like they'll be doing so much they won't have time to do any work?"

"A system is only as good as its users. I'm looking to get the best from what you've got – and some of your people are not using the CAD system properly."

"And what's this CRM you've got here?"

"Customer Relationship Management."

"I read somewhere recently they were overrated," said Robert.

His sister gave him a withering look.

"Depends on what you want it to do and making sure you use it properly. I'd like to design a simple, easy-to-use, bespoke system that will deliver what you want with minimum intervention."

"In English, love, please," asked her father.

Kate sighed.

"Look, this new upmarket design and paint idea you've got. Well the relationship you build with this type of client will be crucial. You need a system that will help you manage those relationships. For example, Sir Joe Bloggs breaks one of his wife's precious dinner plates. He rings you, you need to be able to find out quickly, the design, colour and spec, and be able to reproduce one so that he can replace it without her knowing. *And* when he casually mentions it's their golden wedding in two years' time and is thinking of a commemorative plate, you need a method to flag it up nearer the time so you can remind him and offer some suggestions. Or even..."

"OK, OK, we get the picture," laughed Robert.

"And," continued Kate, undeterred, "I'd like to start considering some e-sourcing tools."

"Bloody hell!" said John. "We gave birth to a computer nord!"

"I think you mean 'nerd', Dad," said Robert.

***

"Ali, I'd like you to meet Kate, my sister."

"Ah, the computer expert. A pleasure to meet you. No, please don't stand up. My wife always found this stage in her pregnancies most cumbersome."

"Have you many children?" asked Kate.

"Four. All boys and a handful! Sara was hoping to return to her law practice when our youngest starts school in September, but she is having second thoughts."

"I'm not sure I could juggle four children and work!"

"Shall we get on?" Robert was starting to get impatient with the baby talk.

"Of course." Ali pulled his chair up to the table and removed a laptop from his case. "I was very interested in this CRM system of yours, Kate, I think it ties in very nicely with this idea of getting closer to customers."

"That's the idea. If we are offering bespoke service we need to have bespoke knowledge of our clients, if you get my drift."

"Indeed, how you use the system will be vital," said Ali. "The equipment you buy will contain explicit knowledge, but how you use it will be part of your tacit knowledge. Can I explore a little with you the features you intend to incorporate into it?"

Robert watched with interest as Ali and Kate launched into an in-depth discussion that quite quickly lost him. He had to admit that his sister had impressed him. Kate had been a bit sniffy about the idea of a consultant, especially one who might have something to say about her own field of expertise, but Ali managed to defer to her specialist knowledge, whilst at the same time showing that he understood what she was talking about.

"Don't you agree Robert?"

"Sorry Ali, what was that?" Robert focused back on the conversation.

"Kate and I have agreed that it is important that you weigh the cost of the new equipment you are buying very carefully. Remember, what you buy must be able to link through to what you do and then through to what you sell. Ultimately the bottom line is creating enhanced customer capital. It's pointless buying anything just for the sake of it and timing is everything: what you are buying will go down in price eventually so you must ensure the price you pay will be commensurate with the level of competitive advantage it gives you."

"Dad will be your friend for life Ali, if you can put a curb on Kate's spending," Robert laughed.

"Spoil sports!" said Kate.

New Technologies: Roadmap for Action

It is Terrisons who are calling the tune concerning Pylgrim's technology capability. It is not a question of whether or not we wish to offer online capability for a customer, but whether or not they want it that counts. Of course Robert has to weigh up the investment against future income streams. The trick is to acquire the knowledge to delight Terrisons and then leverage that same knowledge for the benefit of other customers.

The trigger experience...

A UK cider maker who supplies the supermarket chains, recently had their ICT system down for two days. As a result of a telephone call from the senior buyer of one chain, they were advised that their trading status had changed from colour green to orange.

They were also advised that should the system remain down for a further three working days, then the colour would change from orange to red. At that stage the supplier was informed that they could remove all their cider products from all the stores.

Cider, even branded cider, is a product that is effectively going down in value. They make cider in France, Belgium, Poland and so on. The supermarket chain acknowledges the value of the brand, but what they need more than that particular brand is service. Service online and service offline.

The synergy between Kate and Ali enables analysis of the benefit of the new CRM system. This may fundamentally change the way in which Pylgrim's are able to communicate with their key customers.

...this experience leads to thoughts...

Many business decisions used to be made internally by the directors looking from the inside out, and the impact on the results was sometimes incremental. Decisions today are often instigated externally by customers who want more for less, competitors who are doing it better and the market place. When information can travel at 186,000 miles per second the impact can be, and often is, exponential.

Understand how new technologies will have a direct impact on the performance of your business. Imagine a list of organisational weaknesses that could include:

Out of date, poorly designed website

Lack of effective customer database

No customer satisfaction data expressed in percentages

No system for regular contact with key customers

Cumbersome management information systems

Absence of knowledge of competitor IT capability

Once the bull's eye for an organisation has been signed off by the senior management team, we need to recognise that the very first key change project may be new technologies.

Spend some 80 percent of your thinking time in the future. Specifically, in technology terms, you are trying to work out what customers are going to want, what competitors are going to be offering and what the market place is likely to be doing.

Recognise that it is new technology that is fundamentally underpinning the global economy, so the better we use it the better we will be able to compete. So, for example, the latest range of Sanyo projectors is due to be superseded nine months down the line! Typically, some updated products will be lighter, more powerful and cheaper to buy than their predecessors.

...thoughts lead to decisions and action...

Attend the discussion forums, events and seminars involving technology developments that could impact the business; be at the industry conference or reading the latest research. Who will predict how technology could affect our organisation in the next few years? It is the leader's job to have a go.

Remember that technology itself is explicit knowledge but how you use it could be tacit. If you find ways of using the technology not thought of by the manufacturer don't give it away until you've created and developed your competitive advantage. Pylgrim's have a CRM system designed by Kate and they could use it to send a CAD drawn picture of a commemorative plate to Lord Hawley as a marketing tool and so on...

Deal with an expert in new technologies you trust, since they can find answers using their tacit knowledge. Understand the value of what you are buying compared with the time and energy it takes to learn the knowledge yourself. Learn the language and understand the concepts. Although John, and Robert to a certain extent, find the new technologies difficult, they are wise enough to delegate the work to people they trust.

Recognise that sometimes what is right for the organisation is at variance with what the leader wants personally. If this is the case, as we have said earlier, there is an urgent need to produce a bull's eye, not just for the organisation, but for the managing director too. Both bull's eyes need to be in alignment for success at the highest level.

...so how can action lead to transparency?

Acquire the technology when there is a clear link between the cost of the purchase and adding value or reducing costs for customers. If valued customers 'want it now', we need to have the capability to get the design out and produce results and outcomes in line with customer specifications and deadlines. Alternatively they may be one click away from someone who can. Pylgrim's recognise this need only because the relationship with Terrisons is becoming more transparent.

An example of the TK Factor™ business development process

Siblings can develop powerful and positive relationships or they can destroy a family business with distrust, rivalries and hidden agendas. Robert and Kate are fond of each other; there is mutual respect and trust, which is a great start for their working relationship. Kate is investing in considerable explicit knowledge with the new technology; she will need to share her thinking with colleagues. Her new CRM system is intended to improve dialogue with customers, to break down barriers and develop long-term relationships. The reward for customers is that they will be clearer about Pylgrim's core competences and how they can use them to achieve their own bull's eye.

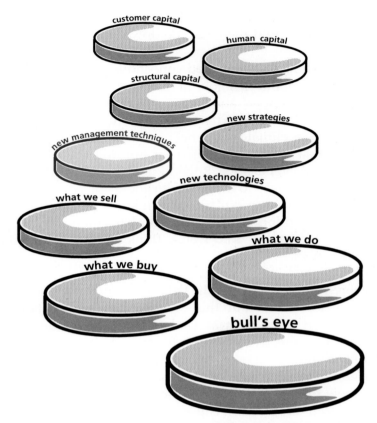

Chapter Six: New Management Techniques

Robert thought hard. The silence in the room was thick and tense – like a summer storm waiting to break.

At last he spoke.

"Having my position constantly eroded, I suppose."

Ali Shah looked steadily at Robert. John's face took on a red tinge and Derek stared out of the window.

"Explain further, Robert," said Ali.

It was halfway into Robert's appraisal; the first one of the programme for the whole of the senior management team initially, which would then cascade down through the organisation as a whole.

Ali's question had appeared innocuous: what had Robert disliked most about his job in the last year? Robert had considered a variety of anodyne answers but had eventually come out with the truth. What was the point of doing anything else? In this new climate of openness and honesty; and with the realisation that if he just carried on burying the real issues, nothing would ever change, Robert knew that he needed to say these things if he was to move the business on.

"He doesn't need to explain – we all know what he is trying to say," blustered John, anger sharpening his tone.

"Let the lad speak," said Derek, thinking of pouring oil on troubled waters.

Robert sighed.

"There you go, 'lad' this, 'the lad' that – I'm not a bloody boy – I'm nearly 33! You all do this – I'm not just talking about the size of my office and the way Dad waltzes through answering questions I've already answered. It's the whole lot of you! I'm fed up with not being taken seriously."

"Well, we need to explore this," said Ali.

"I knew this was a mistake," said John. "Appraisals! Opens a whole can of worms, causes arguments and discord. I managed to run this place very successfully without ever having an appraisal. I own the place – what I say goes! Or at least it always used to." His voice was bitter. "People used to do as they were bloody well told! Now it's 'consensus' and 'consultation' and 'teamwork'."

"Times are changing, Dad, people don't want that sort of management style anymore."

"I know, they need to feel 'valued'. Bollocks!" John exclaimed.

"Robert's right, John", said Ali. "People can choose where they work, they have more options and if they dislike the organisational culture they will move on."

"I'll have you know I always looked after my staff, everyone round here will tell you."

"But a paternalistic culture is not necessarily going to get the best from our people," said Robert. "You take away individual responsibility, if you're not careful."

"The la...Robert's right you know."

John glowered as Derek continued. "Take Josh...we'd a job that needed finishing, offered him overtime, he wasn't interested, but said he was very happy to stop on if he could have time off in lieu. He was here till 11.30 the other night. I was going to stay on as well. He wanted to know why, asked whether I trusted him or not."

Derek paused; they were all looking at him: "Realised I did and went home. Only his word he was here till 11.30, but he's an honest lad, the work was done and done well. Don't get me wrong, he's not perfect – his time management's diabolical and he's always leaving things to the last minute – leaving deadlines really tight. Drives me mad. But even so, I've realised that I can't manage him in the way I used to manage my staff. He doesn't respond to being told; he's creative and creativity doesn't work nine to five. Well so he keeps telling me! And with Irene working freelance, I can't manage her in the old way either. Trust plays a huge part in what I now have to do."

Robert looked at Derek. "You're right, Derek, we do have to change what we do. Flexi-time was one of the things I wanted to discuss with the senior management team."

"But let's get back to your frustrations, Robert." Ali brought them back on track.

"Look, for my part Robert," said Derek, "I'll try harder to remember you are MD and not the spotty kid that used to come and follow me round in the summer holidays. I know I slip back into treating you as I used to and I need to get out of that habit."

"What about you, John?" asked Ali.

"Oh, I get a say do I?" John's tone was belligerent.

"Dad, please..."

"For goodness sake, John, act your age!"

John looked at Derek in surprise.

"What...?"

"Do you want to reduce your working week or not?"

"Well, yes..."

"And do you want Robert to take on the business and grow and develop it into something he can pass on to your grand-children and future generations?"

"Of course I do."

"Then for goodness sake, let him get on with it!"

There was silence in the room. John looked stunned. Robert glanced at Ali, who had remained calm throughout these exchanges.

"Do you trust your son to carry on what you have started?" Ali asked John. "It's very simple."

John thought for a moment. "Yes, I do," he said, at last.

"Then I have to agree with Derek, we need to develop a strategy that'll allow him to do so," Ali said. "Now then, Robert, your development points..."

***

Robert was alone in his office. He sat back in his chair and ran a hand through his hair. That meeting had been very tough at times, but worthwhile. He was moving offices next week; the next SMT meeting would organise a strategy for his father to really let go of the reins; and he had three development points. Robert had a feeling Ali would not have let him out of the room without them!

So, one down and four to go, and that was just the start. If the others' appraisals were as gritty, there would be hair flying, but at least things would change. As Ali had said, a nice cosy chat would not achieve anything in terms of any individual's personal development and that would result in the whole business bumbling along as before.

Robert looked at the Performance Review Sheet in front of him. He needed to network more and get closer to his customers – especially the key clients; he needed to be more assertive – if he disliked the way he was being sidelined he had to take a measure of responsibility in changing that; and he needed to grow into the MD role. Ali had recommended an IOD course for managing directors to help him take on the mantle.

So, it was John next, then Derek and finally Malcolm and Ruth. Robert hoped that there wouldn't be fireworks. But it was helpful to have Ali involved. He had an amazing capacity for getting to the heart of the problem but seemed to manage to keep everyone calm at the same time. Or at least as calm as anyone as volatile as Robert's father could be when his whole value system was questioned. Still, the change in him during the appraisal had been particularly spectacular – something Ali had called a paradigm shift.

***

"Hi, can I come in?" Kate was peering round his door. "Not interrupting anything?"

"No, come on in."

Kate sat down. "Well, the jungle drums are pounding. What's all this I hear, Dad moving out of his office? How did you manage that?"

Ruth tapped on the open door.

"Here you go, Robert, I've typed up these development points as you asked. What shall I do with them now?"

"Pin them up on the notice board on the landing, would you please, Ruth."

Kate and Ruth looked at him.

"What are you staring at? How can I expect all my staff to do their appraisals if I'm not prepared to share my development points with them?"

"Do I have to pin mine up?" asked Ruth.

"Not if you don't want to – everyone's is confidential, though in a culture of openness and honesty it is recommended that we all share this information – especially the senior management team. But I won't force anyone to."

"Well, if you're prepared to do that, so am I," said Ruth.

"Good on you, Ruthie," grinned Kate.

"And that's quite enough from you, young lady," countered Ruth and marched out of the office.

"Robert?"

"Uh huh?" Robert was looking through his e-mails.

"Do you know, I think I might quite like to come and work here after the baby's born. I've been thinking and Jean Paul and I were chatting last night about it. I think working here would be ideal. Have to say, I've been pretty impressed with the changes here."

"Well, I was thinking of advertising for a part-time computer specialist."

"That would be great! So you think it's feasible?"

"Certainly."

"That's great!"

"I'll let you have an application form when I've got the job specification ready."

"What? I have to *apply* for the job?"

"Absolutely – and be interviewed – providing you're shortlisted of course."

"I...you...I don't believe this! I'm family! I'm your *sister* for goodness sake – I'm a shareholder!"

"Look, if as a shareholder you don't like the way I'm running the company, you can say so; if you don't like my performance you can try and get me sacked. But I'm interested in doing what's right for Pylgrim's Porcelain and that means getting the right person for the job."

"I'll tell Dad!"

"What, you're going to tell on me? We're a bit old for that aren't we?"

"No, I mean, yes. I mean, this isn't fair, Robert!"

"Look, my development points from my appraisal were to be more assertive and to start acting like an MD. That is what I'm doing. By all means, talk to Dad, but he's agreed to let me run the business properly. That means me doing what I think is right."

He reached across the desk and grabbed her hand.

"Look, for what it's worth, I think you're very good at your job and that you have an extremely high chance of getting this one. But we've got to do it right – not just so the rest of the staff can see it's what we are doing, but so that we do the best for the business."

"OK…I suppose I see what you're trying to do, but it does seem a bit unfair, especially as you didn't have to apply for *your* job!"

Robert grinned: "That was the old management for you, made some very dodgy decisions. The new management is going to make some changes!"

***

It was 6.10 that same evening and the building was nearly empty. Ali had been discussing the appraisal timetable of the production staff with Derek and was collecting his bag from upstairs as he prepared to leave.

He noticed the light on in John's office and put his head around the door to say goodbye.

John was standing at the window, gazing out at the building next door. He turned his head as Ali moved into the room.

"I used to own all that you know. Sold it to a computer company when we had to cut back. Bit ironic I suppose, bearing in mind my lack of technological expertise."

Ali came and stood beside him. "Regretting your lost empire, John?"

"Not really, just wondering where I went wrong."

"You didn't go wrong, the world changed that's all," said Ali.

"But could I have kept up to speed with that? What could I have done differently?"

"I don't know that you could have done anything differently. What you did was right at the time. It is how you allow Robert to carry on that's important now. We've discussed the sigmoid curve in terms of the business, but you need to consider it in terms of your personal development."

"How do you mean?"

"It is time you started a new sigmoid curve of your own. Look you're still young in today's terms. You've given everything you could to this business and part of letting go is you deciding how you want to spend the next 10 years or so. A personal bull's eye if you like."

"Well I'd like to get my golf handicap down, spend quality time with my grandchildren, the sort of time I missed out on when my two were young because I was too busy with the business."

"Go on, what else?"

"Travel. There's a lot of places I would like to see."

"Whilst you're still fit enough to enjoy them."

"I suppose."

"Everything has its time John. You had your turn and now its Robert's turn. You must celebrate what you have achieved and have the wisdom to move on when you can no longer give the business what it needs. No regrets for what might have been, just rejoicing for what was and is."

"So how do you suggest I go about it?"

"Let's do a job description for your new role as chairman, so you know and Robert knows exactly where your authority begins and ends. Then we'll decide how many days you'll come in and stick to them. No popping in to see how things are going! And then we'll put together a strategy for your personal time. You mentioned your golf club was looking for a new captain. Perhaps you should stand."

"I've often thought about it but it takes up so much time…"

"Precisely, that should see to a least a couple of days a week!"

John gave a snort of laughter. "And next I suppose I pop down to the travel agents and book a holiday to Zanzibar?"

"If Zanzibar will have you, by all means!"

John looked back out at the gathering dusk. "Still feels painful though, Ali."

"Loss is painful. But you're making the right decision and Robert is eminently capable of building on your great success. Just trust him and look at this as a new beginning for you."

"Don't suppose you've got an attractive sister interested in companionship and travel have you?"

"Indeed I have. But I'm afraid her husband might object!"

Instant Impact Diagnostic Tool

Possible comments at Pylgrim's Porcelain Ltd

Person commenting	On	Positive statement	Development point
Robert	Robert	My commitment and enthusiasm	I need to be more assertive
Robert	Derek	Willingness to take on new ideas	Needs to develop greater financial awareness
Robert	John	Experience and knowledge	Needs to trust me (Robert) and let go more
Robert	Malcolm	Not afraid to challenge others	Needs to share more of his expertise with others
Derek	Derek	I have a lot of experience in the trade	I need to accept help from others more readily
Derek	Robert	Has the makings of a good leader	Not ignore 'older heads'
Derek	John		

New Management Techniques: Roadmap for Action

The 360° appraisal, starting with the managing director, is one of the most powerful ways of changing what goes on at the very top of organisations very quickly. It requires courage and humility; it requires leaders to be convinced that every one of us has development points, things that we can do better in order to improve personal and organisational performance.

The trigger experience...

An adviser was attending a board meeting of a nationally known advertising agency. It became apparent that tensions between the female marketing director and the male managing director were hampering progress. They had already refused to submit to a formal appraisal process.

The board (two male, two female) were invited by the adviser to abandon the agenda for the afternoon in order to agree the ground rules for an instant impact diagnostic tool. Please see the model on the left.

The exercise was half an hour old when Jayne (marketing director) was invited to share her development point for Mark (managing director) with the group. She thought for a moment and then quietly said, 'In all my working life I have never been so insulted and humiliated by anyone more than you Mark.'

The atmosphere was electric. The adviser explored this comment a little more and then suggested that they do some further work together using transactional analysis as a model. When both parties understood more fully how and why they behaved in a certain way in certain situations, it was the start of a whole new and extremely productive chapter in their working relationship.

The power of Robert's appraisal is that it will transform his working relationship with John and possibly with Derek and Malcolm also. This work nearly always needs external facilitation if the real jugular issues are to be discussed. You can discuss anything under the sun, providing it is in the interests of Pylgrim's and is done in a constructive way.

...this experience leads to thoughts...

Don't just talk the talk, or even walk the talk, but consider that genuine leadership is about living the talk in all aspects of our life. This means our family, our work, our community, our social and leisure activities.

Consider how you will make time for best practice work. Appraisals or personal development reviews take time but they get better and take less time with practice. Successful leaders create time for activities that are important but not urgent. Such activities also include a range of effective meetings that not need to start and finish on time but also need SMART action points matched to a set of initials belonging to the individual who has taken personal responsibility for delivering agreed outcomes.

Prepare to deal with anger and hostility; emotions that can accompany some key change projects. If high emotion occurs at the most senior level then refer those same people back to the bull's eye that was signed off by them. It is how we handle these issues that can really define our leadership style.

...thoughts lead to decisions and action...

Decide to share your development points arising from your appraisal with your people and it will act as a catalyst for all employees to see learning in a positive way. After all, if it is good enough for the boss, it is good enough for anyone! Robert has even decided to put his on the notice board for everyone in the company to see.

Commit to training. Most serious managing directors do a minimum of 20 days' learning a year. Increasingly, some of this time includes personal one-to-one coaching.

Use (don't just pay lip service to) the life enhancing models that are just as effective in our personal life as they are in our business life; they can include new ways of communicating or meeting, new ways of thinking and creating ideas, new ways of linking or collaborating with others. In an age when the work–life balance is being taken very seriously by enlightened leaders there can be a double benefit from investing in this work.

Do activities that help develop relationships between individuals. People need to be trustworthy. Trustworthy people have character – they are reliable, honest and straightforward – and they have competence, which means that they are constantly updating their skills, knowledge and attitudes.

Encourage diversity in your workforce. The senior management team at Pylgrim's consists of four males. This is a weakness. The types of intelligence that will be required in future, new ways of marketing and new routes to market, frequently require diverse perspective input at the highest level. For example, many organisational top teams are male; almost any same sex top team will benefit from a gender mix.

Make your organisation a place that is attractive to go to. Create a culture of people, where ideas and new initiatives are shared; a community of people to work with. The existence of a talented culture at work is a magnet for customers, particularly the sort of customers that our bull's eye suggests we may wish to attract.

Acknowledge and develop your personal maturity. Leaders that are independent use 'I' statements such as 'I can fix this' or 'I will make that decision'. Leaders that work towards inter-dependency, effective working with others, specialise in 'We' statements. 'We need to discuss this together' or 'How shall we deal with this situation?' This is not about shirking responsibility, it is about working with other people's talent and intelligence.

Exploit new relationships such as that between Josh and Derek, they can be the lifeblood of new income streams. Look for the synergy between people that brings talent together – my abilities only exist in that they complement yours and therefore produce something bigger. One and one can make three, four or even five like this!

Adopt the latest paradigm of management that suggests we treat our people as we would treat our very best customers. So John may well have 'always looked after' his staff but that was a paternalistic sort of culture. That is outdated. In terms of transactional analysis – one of the life enhancing models we work with – people today want to be treated differently.

...so how can action lead to transparency? ⊙━

Make time to explore some potentially groundbreaking changes in relationships at the very top of organisations that may require nothing less than emotional intimacy. Openness, honesty, trust and transparency are perhaps old-fashioned words but they have real power in the new global economy so we had best get used to them. Start with the managing director's appraisal!

Allocate not only time but also energy and money to enhancing the quality of relationships between people. Since circumstances are never the same from one week or one month to the next, nor will be the allocation of resources. This is hard work, especially between those that have been working together for many years, but it has to be done. Today, you cannot have people, whoever they are, whose personal agenda is bigger than that of the organisation. Always look for the right person for the job, irrespective of family pressures or personal preferences; world-class competition by definition, will not have your hang ups!

An example of the TK Factor™ business development process

Ali's tacit knowledge has resulted in an appraisal that has

brought numerous issues to the fore. John has complained of opening a 'can of worms', but the truth is that real feelings and heart-felt opinions need to be expressed for long-term improvements in performance. Transparency sometimes causes pain. Ali again is instrumental in getting John to begin to face and deal with his sense of failure. This conversation brings intimacy between them and this may well be the catalyst for John to follow through on his new Sigmoid curve (see page 50). The reward for Pylgrim's will be a smoother transfer of power from one generation to the next.

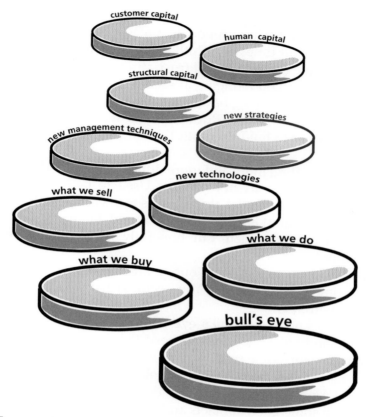

customer capital

human capital

structural capital

new strategies

new management techniques

new technologies

what we sell

what we do

what we buy

bull's eye

Chapter Seven: New Strategies

"Oh, you're actually in work, are you?" Kate wandered into Robert's new spacious office and eyed him with disapproval.

"Hi Kate," Robert looked up at his sister. "What can I do for you?" He was sitting at his desk, typing on his laptop.

"Like the suit. Armani?"

Robert leaned back in his chair.

"Are you trying to pick a fight about anything in particular or have you just chosen me as some sort of scapegoat to vent your spleen on?"

Kate sat down.

"I've been trying to get hold of you all morning. I am hot and fed up with lumbering around like a beached whale. I have phoned you eight times and Ruth said she would let me know when you came in. So, it is a bit frustrating to wander past your door and to find you lounging at your desk, and I had no idea you'd arrived. How long have you been here exactly?"

"About half an hour – Ruth said you were looking for me and I asked her to hold fire until I'd had time to look at my e-mails. Sorry."

"You are getting more and more difficult to get hold of – and what's with the smart new image? Used to be hard enough getting you into a suit, let alone one as well cut as that!"

"Tell me about it! Needs must, I'm afraid. I know it seems as if I'm not around much, but hopefully that will get better eventually."

"But Dad never had to be out so often and I thought Irene was liasing with Terrisons. You seem to have meeting after meeting with them."

"As you know, our bull's eye is about exceptional quality and outstanding service and the need to increase turnover. We need to develop some really key clients, like Terrisons, and we need to look after them. I've been going out with Gerald quite a bit and Ali has encouraged me to do more networking. I have developed some good contacts and leads through that!"

Robert grinned. "Anyway, I'm not sure Dad is exactly the role model I would use in defining best practice!"

"He was right at the time!"

"Yeah, I know, in the old days you could just sit and wait for customers to phone in with an order. You could give them shit service and they still came back. Not any more."

A tap at the door heralded Ruth's entrance.

"Ah Kate, you've found him. Robert, Bob Wright from Dalgliesh and Lyle has been on the phone. Very interested in your ideas for hand-painted customised dinner services and would like to meet up for a chat."

"Thanks Ruth – that's brilliant!"

"You're down in London next Thursday anyway, so I've arranged for you to see them at 2.00 p.m. I'll put together a pack for you to take, OK? Cup of tea, both of you?"

"Please, Ruth."

"Yes, thanks."

"I'll put the kettle on." She bustled out.

"There's a case in point. Met Bob Wright at a dinner, just mentioned this idea I had, then saw him again at another do; he had his MD with him that time. Then I met up with him again at that conference I went to last month."

Kate snorted: "Conference my foot – big piss-up more like!"

"I'll have you know it was jolly hard work. I didn't get to bed before 3.00 a.m. every night."

"I rest my case!"

"And let me assure you, I was not hobnobbing with the people I'd have chosen, but with Ali's 20 – and finding them was even..."

"Ali's 20? Who are they – a pop group?"

"It's the 80:20 principle – 20 percent of the people you network with will add 80 percent of the value to your business. Problem is finding the 20 percent!"

"I'm sure that took vast quantities of beer!"

"Mock if you wish, but I can assure you it is time consuming and challenging."

Ruth came in with the tea. "Gerald would like to see you when you've got a minute."

"Tell him I'll be with him in 10 minutes. Now Kate, what did you want exactly?"

***

Gerald Seymour had worked in sales for Pylgrim's for eight years. He was in his early forties, good looking and charming with it. All the girls in the factory were madly in love with him, but he was totally devoted to Kathryn, his wife, and their large brood of children.

Robert told him about Dalgliesh and Lyle.

"That's great, Robert, well done! Sales are really looking up and a lot of that's down to you."

"What has impressed me, Gerald, going round with you, is how much your customers like you – you seem to have a real rapport with them."

"Well, I've always said there is nothing like personal service, and they have loved meeting the MD – makes them feel very valued."

"Tell me more about this idea of yours."

"You know we were talking about finding ways of leveraging knowledge and building our brand? Well, I was at the NEC last weekend with Kath – it was the Good Food Show. Anyway, turns out that Kath was at school with Mark Jarvis, you know, the celebrity chef! Very fishy! So, to cut a long story short, there we were chatting to him and scoffing salmon and lobster paté on chargrilled crostini. Jolly nice they were too! I think the piquancy of the lemon and chive dressing really made it work! When I suddenly thought that we could work with Mark to develop a range of tableware especially for fish dishes."

"What a great idea!"

"So I took the liberty of mentioning the idea to him..."

"And...?"

"He thought it was a fantastic idea! Jumped at it! Started coming out with all sorts of fishy notions – platters, chowder bowls even ceramic-handled cutlery. Perhaps with a bit of a Mediterranean feel to it."

"Well done Gerald, that's pure inspiration!"

"And a bit of luck."

"Luck is one thing; capitalising on it is quite another. Good old Kath, she hasn't got any other celebrity acquaintances hidden anywhere, has she? No chance she dandled Wayne Rooney on her knee, is there?"

"Afraid not! Anyway, he's coming in to see us sometime next week – so if you could give me some dates when you're available, I'll give him a ring."

**

Later that day, Robert was discussing the project with Derek. "Do we have the staff to cope with it, though?" Robert queried.

"Well as you know I've got a modern apprentice starting next month – damn good scheme, that. And take a look at this!" He pushed an application form across the desk. "I need a new warehouseman – only part time. I interviewed last week and this is the one I'm going to offer it to."

Robert scanned through the application form. "Yeah, he seems fine...hang on a minute, is this a typing error? If he was born on this date here, that would make him..."

"Sixty-six. And no it's not a mistake."

"Isn't he a bit, well, long in the tooth?" asked Robert.

"He was by far and away the best man for the job. He was alert, keen, experienced and very well turned out. He didn't quibble about the hours – it says 10.00 a.m. to 3.00 p.m. in the details, but you'd be surprised at how many people start hassling in the interview about when it's likely to become full time. His wife has just passed away and he is finding retirement lonely."

"Okay, but won't he find the work physically hard?"

"He looked a bloody sight fitter than you!"

"Hey, watch it!"

"To be honest, I'm looking more for someone to keep the place clean and tidy – he was a corporal in the army – all spic and span like. I want to get ready for these open days you're planning. He could even show visitors round. He'll certainly free up an extra pair of hands to work on the transfers."

"Well if you're sure."

"I am. Anyway its just part of this good practice you're always going on about. I was listening to the radio last week. Not only is there a skills shortage in this country, but also low unemployment is making finding good people difficult. I'd have thought a bright chap like you would know all this."

"I do! I'm just a bit surprised that..."

"I know about it?"

"That's not what I was going to say – I suppose I'm impressed by how you've applied the knowledge – I'm a bit ashamed to say it's never occurred to me to try do something about it as such, it's just so easy to moan about 'how you can't get the staff these days'."

"Well, I thought I'd better get your mind thinking about the idea before I get to 65 and you try and make me retire."

"I wouldn't dare! Anyway, thought you couldn't wait to roam the world with your Sheila and the caravan?"

"That's as may be. Happen I'm more interested in helping the government out with the financial burden due to the high costs of pensions and benefits. If I can carry on paying income tax a bit longer, that will suit me fine!"

"Bollocks!"

***

"But we won't make a bean out of it!" John was turning a lovely shade of puce.

"Dad, it may seem a tight deal, but with the quantity of stuff we're going to sell it won't matter. This is a real opportunity to sell off the back of Jarvis's name. He's already a brand, a household name. We're going to leverage that."

"But couldn't you have worked out a better deal for us? The percentage we've got is peanuts!"

"I don't agree. This name is going to get us into every department store, every kitchen shop in the country."

"But this isn't our business, this isn't what we do! Celebrities? Pah – why get mixed up with them. We used to be a manufacturer of high-quality porcelain tableware. I know the manufacture's gone out of the window, but to turn it into a bloody…for some fancy cook! I won't have it!"

Robert stood up and slammed a fist on the desk – his desk.

"Yes, you will have it! I'm MD. I have made a perfectly good management decision that's in the best interests of this company. A decision, incidentally, that's in keeping with the bull's eye you agreed to and you signed off."

He stared hard at his father, a nerve twitching in his cheek.

"I know you find this difficult, Dad. I know you'd like to turn the clock back, return to the old ways of doing things. This has to happen. It will happen because partnerships like this, with Jarvis, are the future for this company."

John sat down, massaging his forehead.

"I'm so tired of it all."

"I know, Dad, but you will just have to trust me, hard though that may be."

***

"Thought it was too good to last. All his talk of retiring and leaving me to run the company. He couldn't resist interfering." Robert paced his office still uptight from the run-in with his father.

"You're being unreasonable Robert."

"What? You were the one who insisted he retire, Ali, I thought you'd agree with me!"

"I agree wholly in what you've done, the decision you've made and the assertion of authority over your father. But you are being unreasonable to expect him to change overnight. Give him time. It is one thing for his head to accept the change. It's quite another for his heart to accept it."

Robert sat down. "I don't agree, Ali, I can't back down now."

"No, you're right to be firm. It'll help him to adjust and give a consistent message. Just accept that new habits take time to be assimilated into our psyche and you will have to manage a level of opposition to some of your decisions to begin with."

"It's just so frustrating!"

"I know. Look, tell me more about this partnership with Jarvis."

Robert explained in some detail how it had come about and what the deal consisted of.

"What really pleases me though, Ali, is that with the bull's eye and the communication and closer links with all the staff, it seems to have encouraged a new way of thinking. Six months ago it wouldn't have occurred to Gerald to make the connection he did."

"That often happens, Robert. And you're right, it is a new way of thinking. And you have got to think differently! People get very used to thinking in linear patterns, but new strategies for developing the business require a much more lateral way of thinking, looking at situations in different ways. So instead of Gerald thinking of Jarvis as a childhood friend of his wife's, he looks at him as a business opportunity, a marketing tool, a way of leveraging knowledge, a brand."

"I suppose an old-fashioned route to market was linear also?"

"Absolutely and often, as you put it, in the singular. Now we look at routes to market, plural, and they are often tangential to each other. And if we look at the business from the outside in, strategies may also be opportunistic, just like this one was."

"I think also all the networking I'm doing is starting to pay off. I've made some really good contacts."

"That's great, Robert! So are you ready for your next challenge?"

"You are joking?"

"Of course not. I think it is time you started to do a bit of public speaking."

"Oh shit!"

New Strategies: Roadmap for Action

It is clear that Robert is seriously starting to change what he does. He recognises the need for the company to be much more visible with important customers than it has been before. Some MDs find the concept of networking and customer visits tiresome, they would much rather be working out a problem, or researching some new project.

The trigger experience...

The managing director of a small brewery was encouraged by his adviser to develop his public speaking skills. (A tape recorder is all you need.)

He managed to persuade the organisers of a National Brewing Conference at the NEC in Birmingham to give him a slot. It was to be an anecdotal story of his company's journey from making beer in a bucket to their present status as an award-winning regional brewery.

Unbeknown to him the CEO of a major supermarket chain was in the audience. The rapport that they went on to develop ensured that the brewery eventually moved from regional to national recognition.

Note the vital connection Gerald made with the celebrity chef. Remember that the bull's eye process invariably requires us to make higher, better-quality 'connections' to help us along the flight path to our destination. As Sue Froggatt says, 'a connection is a meeting of ideas and initiatives that can lift a business onto an entirely new plane'.

The notion of 'new strategies' for Robert has brought him into direct confrontation with his father John. This type of trigger experience can mean an entirely different way of doing business; this is often a catalyst for succession issues in organisations to be brought forward sooner rather than later. Part of what Robert bought by using a consultant was an external perspective to help navigate through these tough and sometimes painful issues.

...this experience leads to thoughts...

Recognise that traditional connections between consumers and suppliers are changing rapidly. It isn't just the advent of technology that makes customers so receptive to forming new links, but deregulation, loss of tariffs and quotas have made all old relationships potentially up for renewal. Think of what banks and other financial institutions are trying to do.

Accept that what we are selling is changing. Even products need to have added value in the form of better service, and this process itself invariably requires us to look for new routes to market.

Think of the people, stakeholders in your life that matter to you – your financial adviser, your website designer, your optometrist, your life coach, and so on. We actually want to hand chunks of our lives over to people that we can trust. For many of us it is a better use of our resources to concentrate and specialise on what we do best.

Recognise that whilst complexity in this life increases, consumers want to simplify their lives more. If this is true for us, then it is true for our customers. This means that simplicity really does have an increasing value; our new strategies must make it easy for our customers to get what they want from us, how they want it and when they want it.

Accept that both financial and physical assets are becoming more and more difficult to leverage – a high-speed train running from London to Edinburgh, for example, can only work one route at a time, however fast it travels. A train reservation system on the other hand, is only limited by the number of people in the world who want to use it.

...thoughts lead to decisions and action...

Get out into the market place and try to look at your organisation from the outside in. Never fudge these issues and if in doubt always use trusted outside facilitation to help give you a fresh perspective on the business.

Delegate this work at your peril; the managing director is best placed to do it because, as Sue Froggatt says, it is not who you know that counts, its who knows you that matters more!

Develop a brand identity, even if you are small or niche. Research suggests that the amount of time we spend pushing a supermarket trolley down the aisle has dropped in the last few years. We are perhaps using brands and reputation not just for quality assurance but also to help us to navigate between a complexity of choices. Our customers will be doing the same.

Use powerful language to describe what you are doing with your business. Transparency, differentiation and leverage should become part of your vocabulary. It isn't jargon! These are words that have a specific meaning in the context of the global knowledge economy. The language that we use is a great tool on the journey towards the bull's eye, providing that we deliver.

...so how can action lead to transparency?

Develop a winning knowledge strategy that is an assembly of intangibles that enable you to get closer to customers to make relationships work. This will be a unique combination of personalised service, brand and trust. Once you can succeed with one knowledge idea you can repeat the formula.

An example of the TK Factor™ business development process

Gerald has a heightened awareness of his own unique tacit

knowledge through working more closely with Robert. The new degree of transparency at Pylgrim's is causing a change in culture and this is changing people's roles within the organisation. Gerald has new confidence to come up with an innovative idea that he broaches to the celebrity chef. He has made a judgement and realises he must strike while the iron is hot rather than wait to discuss his idea with Robert first. His openness and enthusiasm with Mark Jarvis creates a new dynamic process between them. Signs are looking good and Pylgrim's could be rewarded with a profitable range.

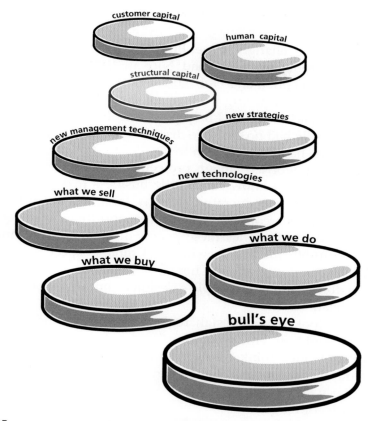

customer capital

human capital

structural capital

new strategies

new management techniques

new technologies

what we sell

what we do

what we buy

bull's eye

Chapter Eight: Structural Capital

Ruth put her head around Robert's door. "Malcolm would like to see you if you've got a moment."

"Of course, send him in – and a cup of tea if it's convenient, Ruthie."

"Not a problem."

"Hi Malcolm, sit down. What can I do for you?"

"Hello Robert, how are you? – not seen you for a few days."

"Fine – and you? How's Irene? We're delighted with her designs for Terrisons – as are they."

"Good, yes, she's worked very hard on them."

Malcolm eased back in the chair and looked around the office.

"Made a few changes, I see. Bit modern for my taste. Very comfortable room, your Dad had. Nice atmosphere."

"Yes, well 'gentlemen's club' suited Dad's style. I think with the customers I am trying to cultivate, I need something a bit more up to date. How can I help you Malcolm?

Robert really had no desire to discuss décor for the rest of the morning – he had far too much to do.

"I'm a bit worried about protecting our designs. Some people Irene and I know run a little business making garden pots and things, very lucrative designs. Well, friends of theirs were in Harrods a couple of weeks ago, and there were some pots identical to the ones these people are making but much cheaper. Rip-offs made somewhere in China, I expect."

"We buy in pots made in China."

"We don't nick other people's designs – anyway, you know what I mean."

"We've looked into design registration before and we do have copyright on what we design."

"I know, but I think we need to explore it further. Before, when our designs were fairly low key and, well, you know, not particularly…"

"Worth copying?"

"No, no, I don't mean that…"

Robert took pity on him, "I know what you mean, not particularly exciting or innovative perhaps."

"Yes perhaps. But with this chef and the designs that may come from that project, I think that the whole question of protecting our intellectual property needs to be reviewed."

"I think you're absolutely right, Malcolm. Let's set up a meeting with a firm of solicitors that specialise in intellectual property. I'll get Ruth on to it. She can make some enquiries."

Malcolm got up to leave.

"Oh, before you go, Malcolm, I'd also like to run another idea by you. The head of the local art college has approached me. She wonders whether we would be interested in funding an award."

"Oh?"

Robert hurried on, "We would run a competition for the best design for a commemorative plate, for that Royal birthday coming up soon. The winning design would be made and sold with all the profits going to charity. Look Malcolm, I know that you..."

"I think it's an excellent idea!"

"You do?"

"Contrary to popular opinion, I'm not so devoid of marketing acumen that I am blind to what is obviously a very good publicity opportunity for Pylgrim's!"

With that he closed the door gently behind him.

***

"So you're an uncle at last!"

"Indeed, Ruth."

"And how's Mum? Your father is full of it. Grandad at last! Grandson and youngest member of the clan, named after him."

"Only second name, Christopher John Richard."

"And Kate's well is she?"

"She's fine. As a matter of fact, I was in there this morning. Just to let her know how well her new Customer Relations system is working, of course!"

"She's gone through I don't know how many hours of labour, just given birth and you talk about CRMs! Did she tell you to go and boil your head?" asked Ruth.

"No she did not. She is a dedicated and committed member of the Pylgrim's team who would not dream of being so abusive to her MD!"

"Yeah, right!"

Joking apart, Robert had mentioned how well the new system was working. He thought all their processes were fairly 'lean', but Kate had made him see that it was a constant journey and that you never arrived. The overhaul of the system had been long overdue and the new CRM, after just a week was proving an invaluable way of keeping in touch with customers. They had even set up a system that would enable them to send a newsletter to all their key clients on the new database.

Kate had gone into labour before the system had been completely up and running and she'd been thrilled that it had all worked so well. In fact, the work they had done had encouraged Robert to look at all their processes throughout the organisation. He had Derek and several of his production people giving everything the once over with recommendations for improvements where they could see them. They were looking at saving both time and money where possible and it was proving very challenging – they had to think laterally, try to look at it from an outside perspective. A real creative process!

***

The phone rang.

"Hi, Robert, Josh here. We've got a problem."

"What is it Josh?"

"Derek doesn't feel very well. Pains in his chest. Refuses to let me phone a doctor. Insists he'll be OK when he's had a sit down and a cup of tea."

"Perhaps it's indigestion."

"And perhaps it's a heart attack. My uncle had one, same symptoms Derek's got. It's not all clutching the chest and writhing on the floor, you know."

Robert made a decision. "I'll phone for an ambulance. Stay with Derek and I'll be right down."

***

A week later and Derek was still in hospital. It had been a heart attack; a mild one, but serious enough to keep him off work for several weeks. And how Pylgrim's was going to manage without him, Robert had no idea! It was all very well doing a knowledge audit of all their processes and systems. What Robert had not realised was the amount of knowledge tied up in Derek's head.

It made him look at John differently too, because he could now see all the little things John still did that he, Robert, took for granted. It was like the oil that greased the wheels, small and not always distinguishable but it was what kept everything working fluidly; the processes and procedures that had evolved and had never been quantified or ever been made explicit. He would have to extract all of it before his father fully retired.

But on the whole, Robert felt good – Derek was out of danger, the new systems were working well, they were well on the way to achieving the latest ISO standard and business seemed to be looking up at last.

He should have known it was too good to last.

"Sorry Robert, we've got a real problem," Ruth was standing at the door.

"What now?" Robert queried. "Not more of the workforce collapsing, I hope".

"Robert, that really is not funny…"

"I know, sorry."

"You need to ring Terrisons. I've had Ron Charles on the phone. They have some concerns about our systems."

Robert stood up "What? After all the money and time we've spent reorganising and updating – they must be bloody joking!"

"They're threatening to cancel their order unless we do something about it – they think that the time between order and delivery is too long and they are looking for a link between their systems and ours – I said you weren't in when he phoned, to give you a bit of time to think this through."

"Surely Kate should have sorted this – I'll have to ring her. At least she's out of hospital now." Robert reached for the phone.

"Should you be bothering her at a time like this?"

Robert glowered at her.

"Right, well perhaps I'll just get on…" She left him to it.

***

"For goodness sake Robert, just calm down", Kate was trying to juggle baby and phone. Robert's voice squawked in her left ear.

"Calm down, what do you mean calm down? They've threatened to cancel their order. Why didn't you see this coming? You were supposed to have sorted the systems out."

"Will you stop yelling at me, you're going to make Christopher cry if you carry on like this!" The baby was in fact sound asleep on her shoulder. Experience, though short, already suggested to her that it would take more than an irate voice at the other end of the phone to wake him up.

"Just explain to me exactly what they said."

Robert related the phone call Ruth had had with Ron Charles.

"Look, don't worry – I told you I'd give you a system that allowed you to develop other applications and that's what I've done. If young Christopher had not made such a sudden appearance I would have sorted this before I went on maternity leave."

"With respect, that's not an awful lot of use to me at the moment."

"Someone I was at university with has just set up his own business. Why don't I give him a ring and explain the situation and he can pick up where I left off?"

"This isn't going to cost me an arm and a leg is it?"

"No, he is just starting out so he'll be very competitively priced, I'm sure. Anyway, he fancied me rotten," she added.

"What shall I tell Terrisons?"

"That there's no problem and it will be sorted by the end of the week, of course!"

Robert swore long and eloquently and hung up.

Kate put the sleeping baby in his cot. "Good job you've inherited your father's placid temperament, my lad, and not your uncle's irascible nature," she said. "One bad-tempered male – well two if you count your grandfather – is quite enough for me."

***

That had to be one of the worst weeks Robert had had in ages. Friday night and he let himself into his flat and headed straight for the wine. Sometimes it felt as if it were two steps forwards, one step back. They had certainly made some huge changes, and Robert was becoming much more aware of the tacit knowledge in the business. Certainly this period of time without Derek had really struck home what was tied up in his production manager's head.

Robert also felt that some of the links were getting much tighter between what they bought, what they did and what they sold, and the new technologies they'd invested in were beginning to enable that process even more.

The problem with Terrisons had been like a bolt out of the blue, but Kate had been right; it had been quite straightforward to fix. But it emphasised this need to be responsive to customer demands and how tightly they needed to work together – all part of the value chain, as Ali would say.

They were now, with the help of Kate's old college contact, linked up to Terrisons so that as soon as stock fell to under a certain level Pylgrim's would be in to replenish. And more than that, Terrisons had to have the utmost confidence that their systems would work. They were now on a trial period and had been given an amber light. If it all went well that would turn to green; if it didn't and it turned to red, there would be real problems.

Anyway, one good thing about the week was that he seemed to be working better with Malcolm who had been right about the need to protect their intellectual property – a crucial part of their structural capital. Though deep down Robert wondered how far one could protect anything, especially with the complexity of protection abroad and what even then you could do about it if someone did copy you. Suing really only seemed an option for the big boys – perhaps it was just about staying ahead of the game.

But he and Malcolm did seem to have reached a new under-standing. He just hoped it would last.

Structural Capital: Roadmap for Action

Structural capital consists of any knowledge artefact; it exists primarily to facilitate the delivery of our core competencies to external customers whilst at the same time reducing costs and adding value for them. Kate is modifying some of the explicit elements of Pylgrim's computer systems that have yet to be evaluated. Derek and John, on the other hand, specialise in some of the tacit elements of everyday processes – things they both do and may have done for years without even thinking about it.

The trigger experience...

A UK components manufacturer was getting good feedback on their perceived core competencies from external customers. Typically these included questions on product quality, helpfulness of staff, timeliness of delivery and so on.

What they were not asking about was the quality of the online service provided. They were, however, hearing informally from customers who wanted to be able to do more on the website. People were saying that rather than talk to customer services they wanted more technical component data online so that they could resolve their own queries more quickly.

This feedback prompted a revamp of their website in collaboration with their key customers. And now they get comment and percentage scores on this competence as well.

Trigger experiences for Robert are occurring thick and fast; Derek's heart attack, Terrisons' systems issues. We use our tacit knowledge to deal with these events and the better we handle them, in the long term, the better will be the performance of the business.

...this experience leads to thoughts...

Consider that knowledge management is done poorly, if at all, in many organisations. Yet the relationship between people and computing power has only just begun. Whilst technology clearly plays a major role in the efficiency of the knowledge worker, so does personality, behaviour and attitude. You have to want to respond in an emotionally intelligent way to what customers are actually saying.

Remember that structural capital exists for internal customers – employees – since they are responsible for the processes in the organisation. Expect there to be a mix of technology and people that can potentially or actually work to create a competitive advantage for your organisation. In the case of Pylgrim's and Kate she is combining her tacit knowledge with the explicit knowledge of the system.

Accept that many of the old sources of competitive advantage, such as premises and finance, have largely been competed away; the answer to this dilemma is in some sort of proprietary knowledge, something that cannot easily be copied. Microsoft is a good example of this and so is Tesco plc.

Look at a combination of knowledge and physical assets, such as Intelligent Finance in the UK who operate a low-cost mortgage and banking business online from one building. They have forgone a collection of traditional bank branches in favour of a 'factory' full of computers in Scotland. A senior manager told me they have a sign outside saying 'This is what all banks will look like one day!'

Ultimately, intellectual capital, of which structural capital is one part, will become the most valuable of all assets, because it is only through unique knowledge that organisations can differentiate their work from that of their competitors. Remember that in the old manufacturing economy the job programmed the worker. People came to work, picked up their tools and asked: 'How shall we do this job?' In the new global economy, people come to work with their tools in their head and ask: 'What is the job?'. See 'The key changes to the structural capital of organisations' on page 116.

See how Pylgrim's, just like the rest of us, is having to do things faster and more efficiently. Lean manufacture is part of this work since knowing how knowledge or value moves through an organisation is part of the knowledge audit. For example, if Pylgrim's are offering a consultancy service, they will have both procedures and outcomes, but the activity will rarely be linear. Terrisons comes in with a problem so there is a diagnosis and a plan of action. This is a *value shop* – it will be a different experience for every customer.

See how a *value network* could exist, where Pylgrim's collaborates with a range of different stakeholders, such as outside designers and suppliers, creating 'transactions' between these people for the benefit of their customers.

Consider that *value chain* analysis tracks the manufacturing activity in China; inputs through processes to outputs. So for three different potential income streams, knowledge behaves in three distinct ways. As a general rule, the less linear the business process is, the greater is the need for developing knowledge assets.

...thoughts lead to decisions and action...

Measure your structural capital. This involves evaluating the performance of your database, software, information supply, systems and knowledge management from both an inside and an outside perspective, including external customers, stakeholders and an awareness of competitor capability in this area.

Ask your internal customers or employees: 'How well would you score our process for recording and accounting for inventory?' or 'How useful is our monthly management information package in helping you to achieve your key performance indicators?'

Key changes to the structural capital of organisations

GOING UP IN VALUE

Features of the 'new' key
Tiny
Easy to carry
Difficult to copy
Hard to infiltrate
Change at 186k miles per second

New knowledge concepts
Satellite links
Latest relevant technology
Distribution networks
Flexible practices
Trademarked brand
Software
Websites
Networks and contacts
Strategies
Innovation and ideas

Blue Lagoon Hotel

Features of the 'old' key
Often large
Heavy and unwieldy
Easily copied
Easily infiltrated
Hard to change or alter

Old knowledge artefacts
Land and buildings
Equipment
Delivery vehicles
Production lines
Product names
Five-part invoices
Brochures
Adverts
Processes
Tried and tested

GOING DOWN IN VALUE

Ask your external customers questions such as: 'How would you rate our ability to meet your delivery requirements?' or 'How effective is our online ordering system for you?'

Select a representative sample of questions that allows you to establish percentage scores for the quality of your structural capital as a whole. Scores and comments against individual questions are the clue to our strategy for improving structural capital. Remember that 'Feedback really is the breakfast of champions'!

Complete a knowledge audit of your organisation and then look for new ways of marrying people and technology in order to leverage benefit for your customers. That's what John did with Irene, acknowledging the older worker's personal circumstances as well as her talent.

Use problems to improve what you do. Tom Stewart said in his book, *The Wealth of Knowledge*, that real, external, customer-added value frequently forms round an internal irritant, just as a pearl develops and grows around a grain of sand.

Create a proactive approach to developing your structural capital that is constantly looking for new ways to stay ahead of the game. You can expect parts of your structural capital to be copied or poached, yet experience suggests that retribution is rarely a cost-effective option.

Look at your physical processes such as manufacturing or delivery that may be owned or outsourced; they are only for the purpose of serving customers. Terrisons are not interested in the back end of Pylgrim's system. They couldn't care less where the product is made, they are only interested in the front end; in other words, what the system will do for them.

Get specialist advice on how to protect your intellectual property, but accept that sometimes it may be better to just try to stay ahead of the game.

...so how can action lead to transparency?

Recognise that as people everywhere are getting more and more used to the rules of the global economy, whether they are booking a holiday or buying a car online, they do not like barriers or delay, nor do our customers. We have to get our performance right or our customers may go elsewhere. Our customers can be, and often are, just one click away from our competitors. Robert is finding out that the journey towards the bull's eye often means engaging with bigger and better customers such as Terrisons. This in turn usually means that they are more demanding. That is why continuous improvement of our structural capital is a minimum requirement from our major customers. At the end of the day, 'We are what we deliver!'

An example of the TK Factor™ business development process

Derek's heart attack is a reminder of just how much tacit knowledge is flying around in people's heads; it comes in through the front door each morning and walks out at night. As explicit knowledge moves faster, organisations have to communicate their offering to customers more effectively and then be ready to respond to feedback immediately. As Terrisons flag up their concerns, it is Kate's tacit knowledge that is missing. She has a solution, however, and there will be a need to reassure Terrisons that Pylgrim's understand the problem and that they are responding fast enough to the complaint. The reward from a successful outcome will be to reinforce the relationship between customer and supplier.

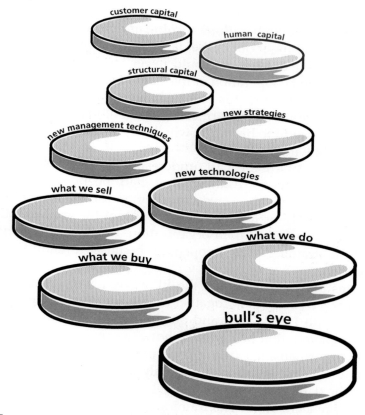

Chapter Nine: Human Capital

Skill, knowledge and attitude – the words buzzed around Robert's head. The work he was doing with Ali was increasingly challenging. It was making him think about the whole business in a very different way; especially the realisation of how much of the worth of the company was tied up in the skills and knowledge of their people. And all credit to his father; he had the knack of nearly always picking people with the right attitude, and then fostering it into a deep-rooted sense of loyalty and commitment to the business.

If truth were known, this realisation had made Robert feel a bit small. There he was smugly congratulating himself on what a marvellous job he had done turning around this dinosaur of a company, pulling it out of the dark ages and blazing a trail to glory; but the truth was he could never have done it without the support and cooperation of the staff. He had taken them for granted, and where he himself had taken the plaudits for the company's improved performance, he should really have been giving more credit to his father who had put the right people in place to allow it all to happen.

In addition, Robert had underestimated the amount of informal, on–the-job training that had been going on at Pylgrim's. Ali had suggested that they go for the Investors in People standard, as it was an excellent tool for implementing good people practice in an organisation. Robert had assumed that little training was happening because it hadn't been formalised.

It was only when he and the IiP adviser were putting the next year's training plan together and the adviser had gone off to work with Derek on it and quickly returned with the plan half completed, that he had seen how, to some extent, it was a matter of formalising existing good practice.

Derek's heart attack had certainly been a scare. With the weeks he'd had off, it had really hit home how much tacit knowledge Derek had. The training plan was proving a useful tool for making concrete plans on how that tacit knowledge was to be passed on.

As for Robert's own training, he had completed the IOD course suggested by Ali – and jolly useful it had been too. But Robert had thought that was it; he had felt a bit foolish when he'd realised that Ali expected his training to be ongoing, and that a certain percentage of his year was always going to be dedicated to his personal development. Ali had told him he didn't want Robert to get complacent and laughed! The Directors' Learning Forum that Ali had recommended certainly looked interesting and he felt he had redeemed himself slightly when he had remarked that he perceived a lot of the value would come from the opportunity of mixing with like-minded people who all had a hunger to be winners.

There was a knock at the door.

"Hi Robert, can I see you for a moment?" Josh's head appeared around the door.

"'Course, come in Josh."

Josh sat down and crossed one lanky leg over the other.

"Training," said Josh.

Robert grinned. "You must be a mind reader, I was just thinking about the training plan."

"Yeah, well I've got some training I'd like to do."

"Tell me about it. As long as it helps us to achieve the bull's eye and you can make a link between the value of the training and us achieving our key performance indicators, I don't see a problem."

"Hey man, you ENFJs are all the same!" Josh exclaimed.

They'd had an amazing team-building day that used the Myers Briggs Type Indicator – a model that looks at individual personality preferences and how they affect our dealings with others. Everyone taking part arrived at a four-letter profile: Robert's type gave him an E for extrovert, N for intuitive – in other words how he liked to pick up information, F for feeling – how he liked to make decisions and finally J for judging – how he liked to structure his life. He liked to be ordered and planned, liked structure and closure, unlike Josh's P for perceiving, which meant he preferred things more spontaneous and open-ended, liked to be flexible and enjoyed that last-minute rush Robert hated. It had helped as well to sort out some of the issues between Derek and Josh concerning the same key area and at last Robert clearly understood why he seemed to rub Malcolm up the wrong way. Malcolm liked the here and now, had good attention to detail, focused on what was real and actual, whereas Robert was always looking ahead, seeing patterns in things – an approach that Malcolm found difficulty identifying with.

It had certainly helped to foster a greater understanding of each other and the *badinage* had continued for weeks afterwards. Even his dad had enjoyed it despite his grumbling about the amount of training being done, compared to 'proper work', and his questioning of how much it was all costing, and why train people anyway as it just helped them get another job at Pylgrim's expense.

Robert smiled, "Yes, well I know what you Ps are like! If I don't pin you down now, it will all be left to the last minute! Come on let's have a look at it."

"Well it's not so much a course as an interactive CD-Rom and additional telephone and e-mail tutorial system to learn French – company called Frenchclasses.com – thought as you were hoping to work with that French client…"

***

It was nearly nine o'clock by the time Robert left the office – the only other car in the car park was Malcolm's red Mercedes. At that moment, the accountant came quickly out of a side door and zapped his car to unlock it.

"Hi Malcolm, didn't realise you were still here."

Malcolm looked up startled. "Oh it's you Robert, didn't see you there – just catching up with some of the paperwork."

"Well I can't criticise as here I am as guilty as you are."

"What's that supposed to mean," Malcolm's bulk looked almost menacing in the half-light.

"Why nothing, just that I am here also working late, despite my clamp down on long hours," Robert replied a little disconcerted.

"Yes, well…best get home." Malcolm slammed the door and drove quickly out on to the main road.

***

Monday morning saw Robert in Derek's office for their regular weekly meeting. Derek no longer asked about John or expected him to join them.

"We've got a problem, I'm afraid Robert," Derek's words hit him even before he had a chance to sit down.

Robert sighed, "Go on, tell me the worst!"

"Ginny Peters and Sylvia Paxman have handed in their resignation – two of my best girls, been here years."

"Why, what's the problem? Is it me and the changes I've been pushing through?"

"No, it's not that…"

"Can't you talk to them, get them to change their minds, persuade them to stay? Have they been offered more money somewhere else?"

"Well no, not exactly…"

Robert started to get impatient, "Come on Derek, it's not like you to be so reticent, what is the problem?"

Derek was quiet for a moment, looked out of his window, thinking through what he was going to say. He turned to Robert.

"Look, this is very hard, I'm not sure how to put this and I certainly don't want to tell tales out of school, but the thing is…"

"For crying out loud Derek, spit it out!"

"It's Malcolm. Thing is, it seems he's been having a…well a bit of a thing on the side, you know, with Tanya Grey in my department."

"He's what? Is this Malcolm we're talking about? You must be kidding!"

"Afraid not, there's been lots of, you know, incidents and it's pretty conclusive. And the thing is both Sylvia and Ginny are very pally with Irene and they feel in an awkward position, what with them knowing and her not and…oh blast, I'm too old to be having to deal with this type of thing."

Robert thought for a while. It explained a lot, especially the somewhat strained atmosphere he'd felt every time he passed through the workshops.

"So if this…er…thing stops, do you think they will stay? What about Tanya, do they get on okay with her?"

"Tanya's still in her three-month trial period. To be quite honest I've had loads of problems with her; she's often late and she slips off places…well obviously we now know where to, but I was thinking of letting her go anyway. As for Malcolm – well perhaps if you had a chat with him."

"You must be joking, this is nowhere in my remit, he'll just think I'm an interfering fool!" Robert exclaimed.

Derek looked him straight in the eye. "Well normally I would agree with you, but the fact is this is affecting the business and, as such, I think you have a right to bring it up. Explain how his behaviour is affecting others. If Irene finds out, for example, then it could mean her not completing the Terrisons' designs."

"Ah bloody hell, you're right, I'll have to do something. Monday morning. Well the week can only get better I suppose!"

***

Robert supposed wrong.

"Calm down Dad, you'll end up in hospital like Derek if you don't just calm down."

It was two days later. His father, almost apoplectic, was striding up and down Robert's office, beside himself with anger, waving a letter around as he ranted and railed at his son.

"Calm down, I'll give you bloody calm down! Malcolm's been with this company for 16 years and now he's resigned. I want to know why and I want to know now!"

Typically, Malcolm had written his letter of resignation to John – just another attempt to have a go at Robert and undermine his position.

"We…ah…disagreed on an issue of company…er…policy."

"You did what? What the hell's that supposed to mean? I want to know exactly what happened. He is a dammed good accountant who has served this company well. How could you let him resign over something so trivial?"

"You don't know the facts Dad, and it wasn't trivial."

"Then tell me the bloody facts!"

"Very well, if you must know, he's been having an affair with a girl in the workshops, two of our best workers threatened to resign and Derek and I both agreed I would have to talk to Malcolm as it was affecting the business. If Irene found out, it could even have threatened the big contract with Terrisons."

"But you can't sack a man for having an affair. Surely something could have been arranged?"

"Dad, I didn't sack him!" Robert got up and poured himself and his father a coffee from the jug on the hot plate. "He took exception to my even bringing the subject up. Said it was none of my...ah...business and if he was not trusted I could accept his resignation."

"Well that's okay then, we can have a chat with him and assure him that we do trust him and that the last thing we want him to do is resign."

"But I don't trust him and I do want him to resign." As his father was about to explode again, Robert interrupted.

"Look Dad, accountants are ten a penny, we might get a part time bookkeeper and save ourselves a huge salary. Ironic really, Malcolm was always griping about the salary bill. We can then get a firm of accountants to help with the complex stuff – the strategy and planning part. Malcolm always infuriated me because trying to get him to interpret the figures was like getting blood from a stone."

"Those women in production, on the other hand, are like gold dust. Their attitude to this business, their whole commitment, enthusiasm and drive are irreplaceable. Neither of them have had one day off sick since they've been here! If it's a toss up between those women or Malcolm, or even Irene and Malcolm, I know which I want. And as for trust, well Ghandi once said you cannot do good in one aspect of your life and do harm in another – or words to that effect. Now I'm not saying that Malcolm has cooked the books or fiddled his expense account, nor am I setting myself up on the moral high ground, condemning him for having an affair. But the level of his ability to deceive us does suggest a lack of congruence in his behaviour that I'm just not comfortable with."

"But he and I are friends, we play golf together! What am I supposed to say to him?" His dad looked old and defeated.

"I don't know the answer to that, Dad, I'm sorry."

"And what about Irene, surely she will leave anyway now that Malcolm's out on his ear."

"I had her on the phone this morning. Apparently she suspected something had been going on for some time and her eldest daughter saw her father with this other woman and told Irene. Irene's left Malcolm and moved in with her daughter for a while – now that the old lady has died she has no ties there, she said."

"What a mess, what a bloody mess!"

"I wish it hadn't happened like this but I have to say I'll be glad to see the back of Malcolm. He had the knowledge and the skill, but his attitude has always been flawed – he wasn't interested in change, just in maintaining his own power base. I can't say I'm sorry he's gone."

"Well I'm glad it has worked out so fine and dandy for you. Does loyalty mean nothing to you at all?" The door slammed as his father made his exit.

"Yes it does, Dad," Robert said softly, "oh yes it most certainly does."

***

"I'm not sure I've done the right thing, Ali."

"Definitely and without doubt! You are right. Skill and knowledge are one thing and can quite easily be taught, but attitude is much more difficult to change. I have another client who always says 'hire the attitude, train the skill'"

"But Dad sees this almost as a personal affront!"

"He'll come round. Remember that when the intellectual capital of your organisation becomes the cornerstone for success, the quality of your people is hugely important. You won't achieve your bull's eye, especially as you talk about 'outstanding personal service' if you haven't got the right people."

"But Dad's argument is that Malcolm's role does not involve him too heavily with customers."

"You know and I know that that is far too simplistic. You were about to lose two of your best girls because of him. There is the domino effect at work here, a strained atmosphere in the workshop affects our dealings with internal customers which will have its knock-on effect to how we then deal with our external customers."

"But we have 35 people working here – can one really make a difference?"

"Come on Robert! You know that it can. I had one client who had 20 staff working for him. One of his most trusted and long-serving members, a girl who had started with him when she was 18, was not only stealing from him, but had a very subtle and subversive way of causing trouble between the other staff. It was not a happy place and I have to say that not even I, coming from an outside perspective spotted what she was up to. Eventually she was found out and sacked. The transformation in the ethos and culture there was enormous."

"One rotten apple, so to speak."

"Absolutely! Look, the links between your structural, human and customer capital make up a huge part of the tacit knowledge you have in the business and that is what differentiates you from your competitors. I once said to you that this journey you are on would either attract or repel people and that you would start to identify people who are on a similar voyage."

"You also said that I might not be able to win Malcolm over, although I thought I nearly had."

"This is not about making easy decisions, Robert. Sometimes our longest serving people need to go and we need to be prepared to do what is right in the interests of the organisation, not for one or two individuals within it, even if they have been there 20 years."

"So values may have to change also?"

"That's right – all your stakeholders need to be on the same journey towards excellence – external advisers, including accountants, as well as your suppliers, customers and staff. Come on, enough of this Robert! No more wallowing! You know you've made the right decision. Surely I have said enough to reassure you?"

"Streuth, Ali, you can be bloody sharp at times!"

"As a needle!"

Human Capital: Roadmap for Action

We may be a great engineer, a superb designer or a brilliant accountant, but our core competencies, by themselves, are not enough. If we want to succeed at the highest level we need to explore some life enhancing models, ones that can be pointers towards fulfilling our potential. Attracting the best people that we can afford and then managing to keep them will be a priority for many organisations; it really does boil down to continuous personal development for everyone on the payroll. Our journey towards personal excellence is manifested by the development of our skills, knowledge and attitudes that we make a habit.

The trigger experience...

At a senior management team meeting in Liverpool recently, the appraisal of managing director, Julia, had been progressing uneventfully until the adviser asked the two managers to consider her 'timekeeping'.

Now 'timekeeping' for a managing director is an entirely different kind of topic than that for, say, an operative. Julia thought for a while. She mentioned the sheer volume of hours she works, including an 80-mile-each-way daily drive from home and she was ready to move the discussion on.

Sheena, Production Manager, asked her why she was always late for meetings. There was a silence. After a pause Julia replied that she had always considered it to be a waste of her time to get to meetings on time. There was even a bit of her that thought it was 'good to keep them waiting'. It transpired how years ago she worked for a purchasing manager who deliberately kept reps waiting as a matter of course. Julia had never revisited that 'old-fashioned' paradigm.

There followed a lively but good-humoured debate. They talked about colleagues' frustration, other people's time and about mutual respect. Needless to say this inevitably resulted in Julia's first development point. From that day on she would endeavour to get to all meetings on time.

Two more crisis meetings for Robert, proving once more that there is risk attached to having transparency in our dealings with people. Whether in our business or personal life two outcomes can result: it can lead to greater intimacy or it can lead to a parting of the ways.

Robert's reaction when confronted with the Malcolm situation was initially to turn and run or maybe to deny that it was his place to do anything about it. Perhaps many of us would have done the same. But Robert thought again, and in another stand off with his father he won the argument and he won the battle; he achieved an outcome that was right for him as managing director and more importantly, right for the company.

...this experience leads to thoughts...

Learn from the way different cultures do things. The 'Chinese' contract for example, is a concept that involves doing a business deal without actually signing anything. Both parties merely shake hands, and if they are smiling the deal will succeed. If one party is not smiling for whatever reason, then the deal will collapse, whatever has been signed. Simplicity again.

Accept the paradox that the solutions to fast-changing customer needs, frenetic competitor activity and volatile market places are in fact a long-term commitment of resources to some 'old-fashioned' virtues and best practice concepts. None of the work under 'human capital' is a 'quick fix' answer to the problems facing organisations

Think of a 'paradigm' as a mental map of the world. In the 'old' economy, it was frequently adequate, not to say profitable, to remain in a 'reactive' paradigm. We could think about the status quo, about 'business as usual', and when a situation arose we dealt with it. The task today is to shift our thinking into a proactive paradigm: to rethink just about everything we are doing in the business, measure the outcomes, receive the feedback, and then think again.

It may seem brutal for the retiring old guard, but the ultimate question for them to try and answer, especially if they are not comfortable with some of the reality of the world we now live in, is, 'Do you want this organisation to still be thriving in years to come?' If the answer is yes, then they are often best stepping aside to allow the new generation to take over.

...thoughts lead to decisions and action...

Having taken the temperature of the human capital in your organisation by appraising the managing director, next sort out the SMT in the same way. In the global knowledge economy, human capital takes on an entirely different, and much more demanding perspective. As mentioned earlier, you cannot overemphasise the link between the skill, knowledge and attitude of the people at the top and everyone else.

Look again at your paradigm of how you manage key relationships; it may need changing. For most of us, we will need to improve in order to develop and sustain a competitive advantage; we have to get closer to people than ever before and we have to let them get closer to us. This requires qualities such as openness, honesty and trustworthiness.

Make everyone link their own development points and training needs with those of their team and ultimately of their organisation. At Pylgrim's ironically, it was only by formalising the training plan that helped them to identify all the informal training that was going on. Skills matrices are an excellent way of helping people to be aware of their competences.

Encourage everyone to really start to believe in 'learning for life' by setting your own example. When people believe that this culture is for real they frequently source their own training as witnessed by Josh wanting to study with Frenchclasses.com

Do something about behaviour. In some organisations meetings start late, have no agenda, go on too long and end up with no SMART action points directly attributable to individuals. Elsewhere, appraisals are poor, working with outdated concepts and failing to result in any meaningful development points, especially for the senior people. Why bother with all this touchy feely stuff? Because when we come up against world class competition, the chances are that they will have done some of this work on relationships already. See 'How well are you and your people growing?' on the opposite page.

...so how can action lead to transparency?

Make the links between each element of this work on human capital. It is part of a whole; it is part of a jigsaw. Intellectual capital is related to the culture of an organisation and the quality of the culture is related to the quality of the leadership. Leaders cannot choose the bits they like, or feel most comfortable with. If they aspire to excellence, in alignment with the bull's eye, then they must walk, talk and live the words themselves.

An example of the TK Factor™ business development process

The relationship between Robert and Malcolm has never been easy. Malcolm is much more comfortable in a world where some things are left unsaid; he is sometimes reluctant to share his knowledge and experience. Robert has a choice: he can allow Malcolm to carry on working with his own limited agenda, or he can continue to develop a culture based on transparency. The synergy between Derek and Josh is working well; Robert can also see the value of Irene and the two girls who

How well are you and your people growing?

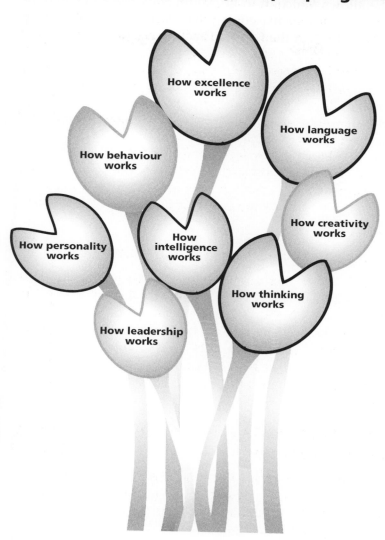

want to leave. Painful though it is, and despite his father's anger, he allows Malcolm to go. Ultimately, Pylgrim's may be rewarded by both increased internal harmony and by being able to look afresh at the finance function within the company.

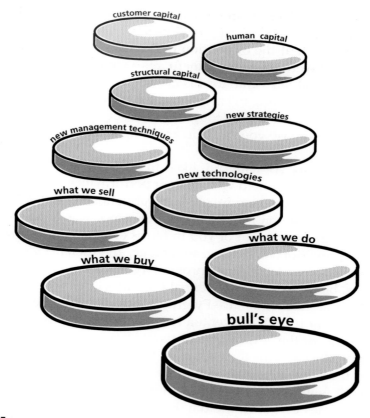

Chapter Ten: Customer Capital

"Well at least you can't say that Ali Shah doesn't practise what he preaches!"

Robert was reading through the client evaluation form that Ali had asked him to complete after six months of working together and endeavouring, with Ruth's assistance, to fill it in.

"And Ali says we need to put down plenty of comments or he will send it back – it is not a happy sheet and the comments are the things which really help him change what he does."

"What's a happy sheet?" asked Ruth.

"Oh you know, one of those evaluations you fill in quickly in the first euphoria of having experienced something and fill in all the 4s."

Ruth looked at the evaluation in her hand. Ali had defined what he felt were his core competences – some seven key areas in which he added value for his clients. The evaluation asked clients to give a rating to each of these competencies.

"It is potentially a very tough process, but you need honest feedback otherwise you can't do anything to improve," Robert said

Many clients, Ali had said, liked to use a questionnaire that gave a rather rose-tinted view of their performance; using it just as an anodyne exercise in self-congratulation. Pointless! The only possible reason to measure performance was to see what your customers thought of you in terms of what you felt were your key areas of competitive advantage, and then decide what you were going to do to improve. Not always a comfortable process, but one that was essential for real winners.

When it had come to Pylgrim's evaluations, the senior management team had eventually come up with two different forms; one for the bespoke, hand-painted range and one for the mass-produced items they supplied to people like Terrisons.

"You realise of course that if we had used the evaluations earlier, it would have flagged up Terrisons' concerns with turn around times earlier in the day rather than left it to the stage where the whole contract seemed to be in jeopardy. Would have saved me a lot of stress anyway," Robert commented.

"Stress indeed – just a modern invention. Nobody ever seemed to get stress 20 years ago and there weren't the time-saving devices around there are now," Ruth remarked.

"That is one of the paradoxes of the modern world," said Robert. "We seem to have less time despite all the inventions that are supposed to save time."

"Well you have got a lunch appointment in an hour, so if you would just stop the chat and crack on with this that'll be one thing off your job list!" Ruth said briskly.

"Me stop the chat, I like that! Cheek!"

***

Two hours later found Robert in a rather nice restaurant, scrutinising a rather delightful looking menu with a rather charming young woman sitting opposite him. Well, work did have some compensation!

"Anyway, as I said, I think this could be a very big client for Dalgliesh and Lyle. He's Greek and wants a 40-place dinner service with his family emblem on it and flora and fauna of his home region. Lots of colour and gold relief. Not my taste but he's the client! In the first instance he wants some design ideas to choose from."

Chantal Rossetti worked for Dalgliesh and Lyle Goods and Gifts, a very upmarket purveyor of luxury items to the rich and famous.

"Well I'm delighted you thought of us."

"You have the reputation of producing good pieces that meet client needs and expectations. The other thing I like is that you are able to source a lot of the materials – I know for instance that you will get the plates for the dinner service and that if any specific design shapes are needed you know how to get something different actually made from scratch. Some of the people we work with just paint, or do design or cast or do the gilding – but you can do the lot."

"It's because of our roots – although much of our whiteware comes from abroad ready for us to print or paint, we still have the machines, the experience and the expertise to produce drawings, plaster-turned models, the block and casing..."

"That's the mould, right?"

"Not exactly, more the mould for the mould so to speak. The moulds that the final piece come from may produce about 30 slip cast objects. But the block and case lasts forever. We still have some of the very first block and cases my father produced 30 years ago."

"Really? Perhaps if the shapes are very traditional, you could use them for my Greek magnate – he is definitely looking for something oldie English."

"When you come and look around the factory I can show you some of the pieces we produced back then. We do quite a lot of tours now and we have some really fine pieces in our gallery. I have to say I'm really looking forward to working with you on this project."

"Ah…well, you will actually be dealing with someone else, I'm afraid. I'm leaving the company."

Chantal turned the full beam of her large, beautiful eyes on him.

"Oh? Where are you going?"

"I am going self-employed, working as an agent and exploiting all I've learned with Dalgliesh and Lyle over the last six years – you know – the connections, the people like you as well as the ones with the dosh."

"How do you mean?" asked Robert with interest.

"There is a big market abroad – the Middle East especially – for bespoke items such as furniture, china, jewellery, all sorts of things, and it will be a matter of connecting the right suppliers with the right customers – acting as middleman so that the client gets exactly what he or she wants. You should have seen this table designed for a guy in Saudi – hand-painted ceramic panels, gold leaf, lapis lazuli, even a jewelled birdcage and bird that rose out of the top!" She crossed one shapely leg over the other and leaned forward caught up in her enthusiasm.

"And when do you leave?"

"End of the month."

"Well," said Robert, "perhaps then you would care to come out to dinner with me – when professional ethics would not be compromised, so to speak?" He smiled.

"Was it only professional ethics you were thinking of com-promising? You disappoint me." Chantal gave him a sultry grin. "Nonetheless, I would be delighted."

***

"Honestly Robert, I know we are supposed to be getting close and intimate with our customers, but isn't this going just a little too far?" Kate gave her brother a sardonic look.

"I really don't know what you mean," he replied coldly, hoping optimistically to deter his sister from continuing.

Fat chance.

"Oh come off it Robert, don't think I haven't noticed how often you feel the need to pop up to London, usually on the feeblest pretext and frequently, coincidentally, making it convenient to stop over the weekend. And then of course it's Chantal this and Chantal that! Really Robert, you're behaving like a lovesick puppy!"

"And you, as usual, are mixing your metaphors."

"Don't think you can put me off, I want to know..."

"There may be lots of things you wish to know, young lady, but at the moment I need to do some letters with your brother." Rescue came in the form of Ruth.

"And just leave him alone, I think it's about time your brother had an interest outside this place."

"Thank you Ruth," said Robert.

Ruth continued, "And I for one will be delighted when he settles down and starts thinking about a family and..."

"Give me strength!" Robert cast his eyes to heaven.

***

Ruth looked at her watch.

"Right it's ten o'clock – let's get started."

The monthly management meeting progressed through its usual agenda items. Ruth was now chairing the meetings, as she was the one who was the most adept at keeping them on track, focused on the key issues, allowed no waffling, no deviation, interruption or repetition and ensured that all actions had a name and due date attached!

"Right, so Kate, you're going to sort that, has that been noted?" Charlie, her new, young assistant, nodded her head and added the point to her minutes.

"Any other business?" asked Ruth.

"Yes," said Robert, "I've been thinking."

Kate groaned.

"I'll have none of that, thank you Kate," said Ruth, "and you're too old to mutter. Please go on Robert."

"I've been thinking about our customer capital, in its fullest sense, you know, internal customers, stakeholders, clients and 'connections' – that network of people who have no direct involvement in the business as such, but who seem to have an affect – some of the people I've met at the breakfast meeting for example, with whom I share ideas."

"Do cut to the chase Robert!" exclaimed Kate.

"Well I think we should have a party!"

"More expense son?" asked John.

"But worth it – look, next year will be our thirtieth birthday and we need to celebrate that, we need to honour your achievements Dad."

"Here, here!" said Derek.

"Bollocks!" said John.

"I think it would be a great idea to get together all the people who really matter to this business so that we can say thank you to them. Past and present. People who have retired from here, local suppliers as well – everyone who has helped make the business a part of the fabric of the community."

"Yeah, you're right," said Kate. "We're part of the landscape."

"Plus all the new contacts and connections, clients such as Terrisons, people like Ali, all the people of the future – we'll even invite Chen Yung over from China!"

"And we could tie it in with the launch of our new Antiquities range," added Josh.

"Now you're talking!" said John, "I do like the way that lad thinks!"

"Well I think it is an excellent idea," said Ruth, "I shall organise it, so you can put my name next to that action point, Charlie. Is that it? Ok, meeting finished!"

Customer Capital: Roadmap for Action

Robert and Ruth are right to explore the mechanics of meaningful external customer satisfaction data. Think of how many 'mission statements' and 'organisational visions' that you have read that include words like 'excellence', 'outstanding', 'the best', 'highest quality'. Yet your experience of their products and services may not have been congruent with the claim on the packet. We live in a world where feedback is the 'breakfast of champions'! This means feedback from both our external and our internal customers and feedback on our stakeholders.

The trigger experience...

A client called in from a motorway service station on his way back from a management development course having spent two days away on the advice of his business adviser.

The adviser had felt for some time that he had been banging his head against a brick wall trying to get the client to change his company's long-hours, aggressive male culture.

The client confessed that the training had finally made him recognise not only the value of his adviser as a stakeholder, but also that the recognition of internal customers would ultimately enhance external customer satisfaction.

On returning to the office, via Damascus, he brought back for everyone on the payroll a £25 voucher to thank them for their contributions to date!

...this experience leads to thoughts...

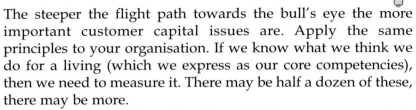

The steeper the flight path towards the bull's eye the more important customer capital issues are. Apply the same principles to your organisation. If we know what we think we do for a living (which we express as our core competencies), then we need to measure it. There may be half a dozen of these, there may be more.

Next consider what questions to ask your customers to discover what they think about the way you perform in these areas. For example:

> We specialise in trying to consistently offer the highest quality of personal service. How would you score us?
> **4 = excellent**
> **3 = good**
> **2 = adequate**
> **1 = poor**
> **0 = abysmal**

To be in alignment with any sort of high-sounding mission statement we need to be scoring 85 percent plus consistently. And even if we pick up 90 percent there will be a clue in the accompanying comments as to what we can do next time to get 91 percent. This is the mindset of winners. As Charles Handy says in The Empty Raincoat, 'Enough is not enough'.

Recognise that it is your 'knowledge workers' who are most likely to enhance intellectual capital. They respect the fact that a hexagonal contract between your organisation includes financiers, customers and suppliers. It also includes employees, the environment and the local community too. If the contract between your organisation and its people does not work or is flawed in some way, then sooner or later the best individuals will move elsewhere.

Whilst the price of products is falling and the value of service is rising, all organisations must try to get closer to satisfying their external target customer needs than ever before. We don't need to ask many questions but the half-dozen or so that we do ask our external customers need to be the crunchy ones! As a general rule the more sensitive the issue facing our organisation is, the more important it is to ask our customers how effectively we perform.

...thoughts lead to decisions and action...

Get really close to your stakeholders also. Too often organisations make do with poor quality, erratic and uncommitted stakeholders. Perhaps, on occasions, that has reflected the performance of the organisation itself. Now that we all have to move towards excellence in order to compete, no less is expected of all the stakeholders. See 'How good are your stakeholder relationships?' on page 144, which depicts five competences that we may wish to consider when we are evaluating anyone materially involved with our organisation.

Make clear to everyone on the payroll what can make them into a winner; this is one of the clues to offering excellence to external customers. With people issues, however, there is no quick fix, there is no magic bullet. This work is long term, just like a bull's eye period.

Decide how you intend to build a strong internal culture and then share this information with everyone. It is only people that ultimately can deliver on any of the challenges facing an organisation today be they competitors, health and safety, environmental, legal or procedural.

Get your people excited about coming to work, about developing themselves within a developing organisation. Charles Handy describes this as the doughnut principal. The core of the doughnut is the essential job, but the outer area is the space available to fulfil our potential.

Use feedback, particularly the comments that accompany the percentages, to devise a strategy for improving performance at every level.

Never be discouraged by disappointing scores, these are

How good are your stakeholder relationships?

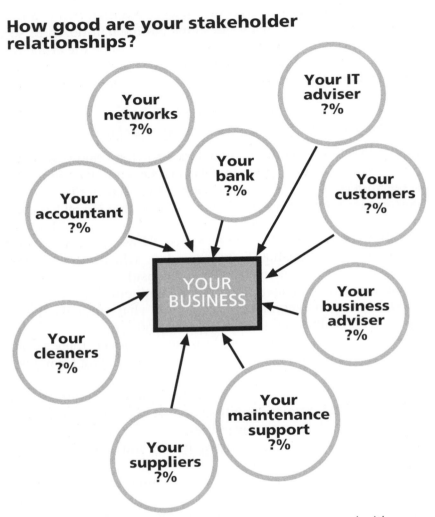

Are these people proactive, competent, hungry, concerned with quality and of good character?
Find a way to measure and enhance their performance for you. **Winners associate with winners!**

frequently the catalyst for the biggest improvements. Poor scores can sometimes mean that you are trying to work with the wrong type of customer; those that would be better off elsewhere. This is why it is so important to match core competencies with the customers you are trying to serve.

...so how can action lead to transparency?

The bottom line is that whether it is internal customers, external customers or stakeholders, the more transparent we are with these people, the more potential there is for a quality, measured relationship with them and the better will be the performance of our business!

An example of the TK Factor™ business development process

As Pylgrim's are working hard to leverage their tacit knowledge for the benefit of their customers, they need to have clear ideas about what makes them special for their customers. Pylgrim's need to discuss, define and amend their core competences as market forces change; they need to get customers to score them, comment and then use this feedback to improve. In the global economy, quality of product is a minimum expectation. It is the quality and speed of service and their unique ability to meet and exceed customer needs that will be the key to their success. The closer they are to their important customers the more rewarding these relationships will be.

Epilogue

It was the day after the party. Ali and Robert were sitting in the lounge of the Belvedere Hotel each enjoying a cup of strong, hot coffee.

"It was a superb evening. Thank you for allowing me to share in the celebration of your success."

"Thank you for all your help, Ali, though I know we've tussled over a few things along the way."

"I've perhaps offered a guiding light; but it's you and your team who have done the hard work and gone through what I know have been some painful experiences. And tussling is all part of it!"

"But we haven't really arrived, have we?" Robert asked. "I thought we'd get to the point where I'd feel we'd got there."

Ali grinned, "No my friend, I'm afraid not. You're really on a continuous journey and your destination can at best be the next milestone, or in this case your agreed bull's eye. From there you review where you have come from, look at where you are now, decide where you next want to be and gather all your resources to help you get there. And often it will mean changing what you're doing in order to reach your next milestone. The truth is that with the world getting smaller and change happening faster, many more milestones will exist in an organisation's life than ever before. The mark for future success of any organisation will be how quickly they can change and adapt to the forces around them."

Robert sighed, "Makes you wonder why we do it really."

"You do it for the same reasons your father did it: for the challenge and excitement! It's just that the challenges that your father faced are very different from the ones you face and those in turn will be very different from the ones your son or daughter will face."

"Hey, hang on a minute, Chantal and I have only just got engaged!"

"And it's probably an excellent time for you to be

considering your own personal bull's eye."

"How do you mean?"

"Now that you are getting married you need to ensure that the Robert Pylgrim family bull's eye is in line with what you want to achieve for the business. Obviously Chantal knows what she is marrying into, and perhaps your connection with each other is partly because she understands the pressures you have."

"Pure luck, Ali."

"There's really very little luck in running a successful business. Good karma, yes, but not luck! You are what you decide to be and the quality of your decisions will be crucial to your future."

"You're right of course, Chantal and I will need to sit down and have a chat. You always make things seem…well not easy exactly, but so straightforward."

"What I do is shake off the emotion from the situation, hold it up to scrutiny so that the decision seems simpler. I offer you objectivity. Take your sister's appointment, for example. If I were to say to you regarding a vacancy for a post, 'Look'," Ali pointed to someone reading a paper across the hotel lounge, "'they seem to be suitable, let's offer them the job', you would think I were mad. Yet that is effectively what many family businesses do. We've got a job, Uncle Harry is at a loose end, let's wheel him in!"

"But it is not quite as…"

"I know, I know it is not as simple as that, but by exaggerating the picture we come up with a principle."

"Wasn't I a bit of a square peg in a round hole when we first met?"

"As I have said to you before, your leadership capabilities are brilliant; you have what it takes to be a winner in the new global economy for a variety of reasons. Firstly, you have emotional intelligence – just as important for leadership nowadays as the analytical intelligences."

"That's a relief!"

"But I'm convinced that your greatest gift lies in the fact that you have the humility to learn and that's wonderful. It is only through learning that we will enhance the intellectual capital of our businesses and that, in turn, will help us respond to the new challenges ahead. You must let me know when you think you have arrived and I'll come and tell you differently!"

"I still want you to work with us – not as intensely, perhaps."

"Of course – I agree, my involvement should now become less frequent. We could agree to meet up every six months, say, to review progress and discuss future options."

"That would be good!" Robert took a sip of coffee. "You know that Dad's more or less decided to retire completely?"

"I suspected he would, he just needed this period of transition to help him adjust to the idea. He was telling me last night how proud of you he is and how much you have achieved this year. You may not be back up to 60 staff, but you're on your way."

"He did? Thank you for telling me that. Funny, I still need to have his approval. To be honest I was afraid he would never trust me enough to let me take over."

"Trust is a strange thing. I don't think it was that he doubted your ability or integrity. I think he just needed to be reassured that you would take on the custodial mantle, as opposed to just the ownership of the business."

"How do you mean?"

"For a lot of family businesses, whether of second, third or even fourth generation, there is often a feeling by the current owners that they have been loaned it, that they just have stewardship of it and a responsibility to hold it in trust for future generations. It is not uncommon for founders to feel that they have created something that will still be here long after they have gone – a bit like having children."

"But is that realistic bearing in mind what we have said about the rapidity of change? Surely these old established firms are no longer viable?"

Ali smiled. "Sorry, I've no answer to that. You know how

long it takes for an ocean liner to turn round? Well if the old economy sustained ocean liners then the new economy requires a speedboat that can zip through the water and change direction in seconds. Who knows where the family business sits with that? All I know is that when your progeny are of an age to make choices about their careers, you will probably be as keen for them to make a success of Pylgrim's in whatever way they have to in order to compete in the future economy – just as your father was for you to take over from him."

"You are probably right. Kate is already planning out young Christopher's education, university course and role in the business!"

"Providing he is successful in his application for the position, of course!"

"Well that goes without saying, Ali!"

Robert continued, "So we need to set up a meeting with the SMT don't we?"

"Indeed, to do what?"

"To review the bull's eye, make sure we are on target and if not what we do about it."

Ali smiled. "An excellent idea, Robert!"

Robert looked at him quizzically.

"Just testing were you?"

Ali laughed.

To be continued...

Glossary

The words we use are so important for conveying meaning, yet we often use different words when we mean to say the same thing. Some words seem similar, yet mean something completely different. Try debt, debtor and debit for example! Below is what we mean by some of the words we use in this book.

Alignment

When all employees from the most junior to the most senior understand what and how they contribute to the organisational bull's eye, they can be said to be in alignment.

Bull's eye

This is a metaphor for what a person or an organisation would like to be at some future point in time, usually three years. Most developmental models suggest that the more clearly we define our bull's eye the more likely we are to achieve it.

Competitive advantage

For a limited company this could mean return on capital invested; for a school it could mean Ofsted grades; for a council department it could be successful funding bids based on performance; for an athlete a gold medal.

Congruence

This is the quality of making our words, our tone of voice, our body language and our actions all say the same thing.

Connections

These are the people who can potentially lift our organisation onto another plane through their own or other people's expertise. In this context, it may not be who you know, but who knows you that matters most!

Customisation

Our customers are increasingly expecting our products and services to be tailored to their particular requirements. The better we are able to do this profitably the more successful we are likely to become!

Differentiation

There are no safe havens for doing business any more. Competitors can appear from nowhere and be doing it better and faster than we can. We therefore need to differentiate ourselves by offering unique tacit knowledge that gives us a competitive advantage in the market place.

Energy (see Resources below)

We are all blessed with varying amounts of energy, but successful people are aware of the component parts that are physical, mental, emotional and spiritual. Peak performance often requires us to harness all four aspects if we are to fulfil our potential.

Feedback

As Ken Blanchard says in *The One Minute Manager*, 'Feedback is the breakfast of champions' and how right he is. The quicker that we get clear, measurable and constructive feedback on our performance the quicker we can do something to improve. This is part of the journey towards excellence that is required to be a winner in the knowledge economy.

Intellectual capital

This means the combined value of structural, human and customer capital. It is the sum of the intangible assets in the form of knowledge that is replacing tangible assets as a basis for creating competitive advantage in the market place.

Key Performance Indicators (KPIs)

Some organisations talk about Aims and Objectives, others about Targets and Goals and yet others about Key Performance Indicators. Whilst the bull's eye is often a three-year perspective on performance, KPIs are usually valid for twelve months and they need to be SMART (see below).

Knowledge audit

This is the process of mapping the knowledge that can be used to create a competitive advantage. The outcome of this exercise will be a unique combination of tacit and explicit knowledge (technology-based) for every organisation.

Leverage

Leveraging is using the same knowledge repeatedly but with little or no increase in variable costs. You may lecture in a college and be paid for the lecture; using the same material you may create a television programme that is seen all over the world and for which you get paid a lot more!

Life enhancing models

We refer to several, all of which are widely documented on the internet. See also the Suggested Further Reading on page 157.
The Myers Briggs indicator – personality preferences
Transactional Analysis – behavioural preferences
The Johari Window – an intimacy model
Paretto's 80:20 rule – a personal effectiveness model
Neuro Linguistic Programming – modelling excellence in people
Lateral thinking – thinking from a different perspective

Outcome

An outcome is the result we wish to achieve from having completed one or more tasks.

Paradigm

A paradigm is a mental map of the world. It is how we view a situation or circumstance based upon our previous experience.

Paradigm shift

This is when we see a situation or circumstance in a very different way to how we used to see it. A paradigm shift can occur in a split second.

Resources

Whatever our journey consists of we can spend time, energy and money to accomplish it. 'Winners' who most frequently achieve their bull's eye are usually highly skilled in the allocation of their resources.

Senior Management Team (SMT)

These are the people that are responsible for delivering the outcomes for the business. These are the KPIs in the short term and the bull's eye in the long term.

SMART

Sometimes pertaining to KPIs, sometimes to Action Points, this is an acronym that can stand for Specific, Measurable, Achievable, Resourced and Timed. Much of the debate and discussion normally takes place around whether or not something is achievable and/or resourced.

Stakeholders

These people include anyone that is materially involved in the business. They could include accountants, banks, cleaners, distributors, website designers, PR teams, recruitment agencies, legal people, in fact any outsourced expertise.

Tacit knowledge

This is the conscious identifying, using and enhancing of tacit knowledge, leading initially to transparency with others and ultimately to business reward.

Task

A task is something we have to accomplish in order to achieve an outcome. The clearer the desired outcome is, the more energy we can bring to the task.

Time (see Resources above)

Time combined with energy and money make up Resources. Successful people often know how to prioritise things that are important but not urgent. Essentially this means taking a proactive rather than a reactive stance to how they use most of their time.

TK Factor™ business development process

This is the conscious identifying, using and enhancing of tacit knowledge, leading initially to transparency with others, and ultimately to business reward.

Transparency

This is the degree of openness and honesty that we choose to have with our stakeholders, our internal and external customers. The greater the trust and mutual respect between people the greater the transparency that is usually possible.

Winner

A 'winner' in this context is someone who is demonstrably on the journey of continuous personal development. A 'winning organisation' in this context creates and sustains competitive advantage in the global knowledge economy. In practice a bull's eye may include needs of employees, suppliers, stake-holders, the local community, the environment, and financiers. It sometimes includes family and spiritual considerations too.

Suggested further reading

Berne, Eric (1964) *Games People Play*, Penguin Books

Buzan, Tony & Israel, Richard (2000) *Sales Genius*, Gower

Covey, Stephen (1998) *Principle Centred Leadership*, Simon & Schuster

De Bono, Edward (1998) *Simplicity*, Viking

Goleman, Daniel (1999) *Working with Emotional Intelligence*, Bloomsbury Publishing

Handy, Charles (1990) *The Empty Raincoat*, Arrow Business Books

Handy, Charles (1992) *The Age of Unreason*, Arrow Business Books

Kapferer, Jean-Noel (2001) *(Re)inventing the Brand*, Kogan Page

Kennedy, Carol (1991) *Guide to the Management Gurus*, Business Books

Kennedy, Carol (2003) *From Dynasties to Dotcoms*, Director Publications Ltd

Koch, Richard (1998) *The 80/20 Principle*, Nicholas Brealey Publishing

Leadbeater, Charles (2000) *Living on Thin Air*, Penguin Books

Mitroff, Ian & Linstone, Harold (1993) *The Unbounded Mind*, Oxford University Press

Myers/Briggs (2000) *Introduction to Type*, Oxford Psychologists Press Ltd

Peters, T J & Waterman R H (1982) *In Search of Excellence*, Harper & Row

Poelje, Sari van & Steinert, Thomas (1996) *Transactional Analysis in Organisations*, ITAA

Risner, Nigel (2004) *You Had Me at Hello*, Limitless Publications

Robbins, Anthony (1991) *Awaken the Giant Within*, Simon & Schuster

Roberts, Martin (2001) *Change Management Excellence*, Crown House Publishing

Robinson, Ken (2001) *Out of Our Minds*, Capstone Publishing

Roper, Peter (2004) *Feel Free To Speak*, Peter Roper

Stewart, Ian & Joines, Vann (1996) *TA Today*, Lifespace Publishing

Stewart, Thomas (2001) *The Wealth of Knowledge*, Nicholas Brealey Publishing

Woodward, Clive (2004) *Winning!*, Hodder & Stoughton